CONFESSIONS

OF A

PROFESSIONAL HOSPITAL

PATIENT

**A Humorous First Person Account Of How To
Survive A Hospital Stay And Escape With Your
Life, Dignity And Sense Of Humor**

By

MICHAEL A. WEISS

D1304375

ISBN: 0-75960-473-8

This book is printed on acid free paper.

1stBooks - rev. 02/2/01

This book is dedicated to my Mom and Dad.

My ability to cope with extraordinary adversity and prosper by laughing, fighting, loving, learning and helping others is a direct result of my following their respective examples.

Of course, I would not have needed these skills if I had simply inherited genes from healthier parents! "That's Life" - and I wouldn't have wanted it any other way. They are my "home" and my upbeat story would not exist were it not for their love, patience, encouragement and laughter.

Contents

Introduction

Why Should You Read This Book?

There are certain unique experiences in life that can only be accurately described by those who experience them. The wisdom imparted by these storytellers in various forms of media are invaluable and help those who follow become more successful than their predecessors. Some of these detailed experiences involve glorious life adventures such as becoming a major league baseball player, preparing for motherhood, traveling around the world or lowering a golf handicap. Others, however, are more fundamental to day-to-day functioning and include descriptions of successfully battling cancer, living life with a physical handicap, coping with the death of a spouse or effectively losing weight. Some of these books, tapes, television programs and lectures are realistic, helpful, informative and well intentioned. But the modern day insatiable appetite for information breeds too many storytellers with unrealistic perspectives, hidden agendas and inadequate qualifications.

Being a hospital patient falls into the category of "day-to-day functioning" experiences but for some reason, despite its probable eventuality for every person at some point in their lives, people don't seem to know the specifics involved and tend to rely on out-of-date stereotypes. What's worse is that some present accounts of the experience are compiled by medical professionals and insurance companies whose viewpoints are completely inappropriate for a realistic description of the patient's perspective. There are, however, also accounts written and disseminated by patients but most of these are based upon limited and often harsh exposure to the experience. These descriptions are therefore often too critical and do not present accurate or useful descriptions of the experience.

1

Because I have been hospitalized approximately fifty (50) times for a wide range of ailments with both successful and unsuccessful medical outcomes, I am all too familiar with the bureaucratic chaos, practical inadequacies and emotional frustrations associated with the hospital patient experience. Having survived these hospital stays and blossomed into a normal functioning adult, I have demonstrated the unique coping skills and techniques required for success as a hospital patient. Due to my patient experience, perspective and professional/educational background as an attorney, MBA and writer, I am able to communicate these skills and techniques to individuals faced with hospitalization in such a manner that they too can experience a similar positive personal outcome. As a result, if I am successful in relating the experience, information and wisdom I have acquired, you will not have to go through some of the unfortunate experiences I have endured as a hospital patient and can focus your attention strictly on medical recovery. That's why you should read this book.

HOW TO USE THIS BOOK

The book is broken down into ten chapters listed in the logical order in which I, as a prospective hospital patient, would search for them prior to a hospital stay. I have also listed extensive chapter sub-headings so that at a quick glance you can see the contents of each chapter and prioritize your reading should your situation or preferences so require. The book is also designed this way to serve as a reference guide should you be searching for specific information.

CHAPTER SET-UP

Chapter 1, "Pre-Admission Preparation," details the practical components of preparing for a hospital stay but also addresses valuable emotional tools necessary for a smooth stay. Chapter 2, "A Typical Day In The Hospital: Welcome To Club Med?" explains what the hospital patient should expect in terms of routine, scheduling and atmosphere. Chapter 3, "Nurses," provides valuable insight into the health care workers with whom you will have the most interactions. Chapter 4, "Physicians," describes the health care workers with whom you'd like to have the most interaction with but for various reasons do not. This chapter also provides a practical explanation of "Managed Care" and explains how it affects the hospital patient-physician relationship. Chapter 5, "Reaching Out," provides some suggested coping techniques with respect to relationships outside of the hospital such as those with family, friends and business associates. Chapter 6, "Dealing With The Inside World," relates suggested coping skills for issues and individuals encountered within the hospital environment such as privacy, death and roommates.

Chapter 7, "The Emergency Room," provides some background on what is fast becoming the frontline of medical care in the managed care environment. Chapter 8, "Bouncin' Back," is a first-hand account of my rehabilitation from spine-fusion surgery and provides general insights into dealing with the set-backs and overall physical and mental aspects of recuperation from the hospital stay. Chapter 9, "Appealing Managed Care Coverage Decisions," provides unique insight into the managed care dispute resolution process from the frustrating start to, at least in this one instance, a rewarding finish. Some of the actual correspondences involved in the dispute process are included in an appendix and can serve as a reference guide should you be forced to take similar measures. Finally, <u>Chapter 10</u>, "<u>For What It's Worth</u>," contains my humble suggestions regarding possible improvements hospitals can implement to enhance the patient experience so that books like this are not necessary in the future.

<u>THE STYLE</u>

The stories in the book are real because I have experienced them. Some are said, some are funny, others are demeaning but I've chosen to share them for illustrative and demonstrative purposes. In trying to sell the initial manuscript, whose working title incidentally was, "One More Rectal Exam And I'm Outta This Hospital!," potential editors and publishers opined that the "hospital patient experience" can be professionally written about in only one of two ways. More specifically, they suggested that the book be either of the "How To" variety or a "Humorous" look at hospitalization. I trusted this advice because it came from extremely successful and experienced executives in the publishing industry. However, my intent was not to get a book published. My intent was to help people cope with situations in which I am uniquely well experienced but I would only get that opportunity if I got the book published. Therein, as they say, "lies the rub."

Since each of my hospitalizations included humorous, dramatic, inspiring, embarrassing, revealing, shocking and depressing events along with a multitude of responsive feelings/emotions, I knew it would be difficult to separate and label my perspective in accordance with the themes suggested by the professionals who were so kind in advising me. I'm sure a "How-To" book on the subject would be extremely helpful but it might be boring to read. After all, it's not like the reader/prospective patient would be as enthused as a prideful Mom buying a "Disney Guide Book" in preparation for her family's first trip to Disney World! On the other hand, I'm sure a "Humorous" book on the subject would be enjoyable to read and possibly would minimize some of the traumatic experiences associated with being a hospital patient but it wouldn't be helpful or realistic.

In the end, I chose to simply be honest and wrote about what I experienced. As a result, the book is both informative and entertaining and most of all it is realistic. However, I also listened to the professional advice and organized the book as a "How-To" guide. To that extent, I have included detailed subheadings so that the reader can use the book as a reference source. I hope you will appreciate my candid approach because you will need to tap into a similar personal resource to survive your hospital stay and escape with your life, dignity and sense of humor.

WHO AM I?

I am a relatively healthy individual who unfortunately has been hospitalized approximately fifty (50) times. To the extent, my body has been probed and prodded by medical students, interns, residents, fellows, nurses, occupational therapists and even by God (or at least that's whom the physicians thought they were). I have law and MBA degrees, maintain a profitable law practice and live a normal life. However, being frequently hospitalized is a part of that normal life.

The hospitalizations primarily began in 1984, when I was 21 and diagnosed with "Crohn's Disease" - a chronic illness involving an inflammation of the intestines. While physician theories vary, the overall consensus is that Crohn's Disease sucks. No, that's not entirely accurate. Physicians generally agree that it is an "auto-immune" illness, it's the patients who think it sucks! As an "auto-immune" illness, its effect is not limited to the intestines because it also wreaks havoc on the immune system resulting in other afflictions that appear to the untrained eye as unrelated to the intestinal problems. With all due respect to Mr. Sinatra, "When I was 21" - it was not a very good year.

My hospital stays range from a few days to several weeks. I am usually admitted because of intestinal obstructions. A physician once described the obstruction as being similar to a "kink" in a garden hose. Sexual depravity aside, the hospital treatment is conservative and also includes boredom, rest, starvation and intravenous medications/nutrients (e.g. antibiotics, steroids, pain medications and vitamins). The treatment theory is analogous to that for a sprained ankle - if it hurts, stay off it. Unfortunately, the only way to do this safely for intestinal conditions is to do so in a hospital. Many times, however, the conservative treatment has not been successful and as a result I've undergone numerous surgeries to fix the "kink."

While my last surgery in 1996 has seemed to alleviate the most serious intestinal concerns, if I were to keep score I would estimate I have had approximately ten surgeries where portions of my small intestine were removed. I would also estimate that I have endured: 75 rectal examinations, 67 requests to "now turn your head to the right and cough," 46 different tasting versions of what is universally referred to as a "hamburger," 92 completely false assurances that "you will only experience minor discomfort," 50 roommates skilled at making foul-smelling trumpet sounds without instruments and 72 temptations to actually buy something from The Home Shopping Network.

These aforementioned surgeries in and of themselves have caused additional surgeries ranging from repairs of abdominal "incisional" hernias to procedures for removal of scar tissue or "adhesions." Unfortunately for me, but fortunately for you and for the purposes of this book, my hospitalizations have not been limited to intestinal problems because Crohn's Disease has also caused several other ailments requiring hospitalizations such as knee surgery, kidney stones and my most recent hospital stay for spine fusion surgery. What started out as a typical "herniated disc" ended up being a diagnosis of "Degenerative Disc Disease." The Crohn's Disease link is that according to my gastroenterologist the degeneration was probably caused by, or was a long-term side effect of, the various abdominal surgeries and/or treatment medications.

So what do I know about the hospital patient experience? I know that it's difficult. I know that it can be physically and emotionally painful. I know that it can be frustrating, revealing, embarrassing, demeaning and dehumanizing. I certainly know that it can be expensive. However, I've learned that if it is dealt with properly, the hospital patient experience can be funny, educational, moving, warm, empowering and motivating. As a result, it can make you a more sensitive, compassionate, understanding and appreciative person.

Just like you, I attempt to live a normal life. As part of that life and despite my medical difficulties, I have attended college in upstate New York (S.U.N.Y. at Binghamton), law school in Boston (New England School of Law), and business school in both Austin, Texas (University of Texas) and Hempstead, New York (Hofstra University). As a result, however, I have been hospitalized in many different hospitals in several different states. Because my hospitalizations have occurred during the past fifteen years, I have witnessed first-hand the dramatic changes to the American healthcare system. These experiences coupled with my educational background make for a unique perspective (not to mention a tremendous amount of debt).

<u>WHY I WROTE THIS BOOK</u>

I'm sharing this perspective with the hope that my outlook, observations and suggestions help people and institutions cope with one of the most probable realities of life - hospitalization. I also hope this book reminds medical professionals of not only the significance of their jobs but also of the importance of their demeanor and compassion. I am not a hospital administrator, psychologist, physician or healthcare specialist. I am just a patient. To that end, I trust my candor will be taken at face value, with good intent, humor and respect.

Chapter 1

PRE-ADMISSION PREPARATION

Practical and Emotional Preparation for the Hospital Stay

Much like staying over at your in-laws, the hospital stay is an experience that compromises your right of privacy, sense of dignity, emotional well-being and forces you to share a bathroom with very strange people. While vodka, valium and constantly saying, "I'm so glad we did this" are the antidote for your in-laws, sometimes all you need in the hospital are "Life Savers," sweet-smelling shampoo and a pair of worn-in slippers! However, a hospital stay could be a devastating experience (although I imagine so could a visit to one's in-laws) and the manner in which it is handled often determines whether or not one recuperates properly, if at all.

As in any other challenging or difficult experience in life, the key to success as a hospital patient is preparation. For a hospital stay, preparation is comprised of emotional and practical components. Thanks to the never-ending barrage of insurance payment foul-ups and medical billing mistakes, there are also paperwork considerations and insurance referral/approval requirements that should be addressed as part of this preparation so as to minimize the subsequent deleterious effects of the foul-ups and mistakes.

9

PURCHASE A COMPUTER

Unless your situation is emergent, deal with the paperwork and insurance requirements as soon as is practicable under the circumstances due to the associated long-term financial ramifications. To that extent, if you can afford one, purchase a computer. If you already have one, utilize it to organize your appointments, letters, bills, addresses, costs etc. This computerized approach to dealing with insurance carriers and medical-billing offices minimizes the inevitable bureaucratic foul-ups, mistakes, miscommunications and frustrations. It also provides a "paper trail" for a loved one to follow should you become too ill to keep up with the paperwork.

If possible, utilize the Internet and communicate through e-mail. We as patients and consumers are now equipped to communicate with insurers and billing offices in the same impersonal manner by which they communicate with us. Fight fire with fire! The biggest administrative hurdle is often obtaining the name of the person responsible for your account. In many instances you will only be afforded contact with a computerized voice-mail menu. In that case, ALWAYS choose the "Rotary Phone" selection! It's your best chance of getting a live person. If you have two telephone lines, leave the internet-accessible line open while you make your medical calls so that you can entertain yourself while being forced to listen to Muzak versions of Beatle songs on hold. Cruise the Net, check-up on your stocks, e-mail a friend or play a video game but do not start humming the words to "Let It Be" because then you will have begun losing the battle against the insurance company. After all, the first sign of submission (and incidentally, middle age) is recognizing a Muzak song <u>and</u> singing the words!

<u>ORGANIZATION IS THE KEY</u>

In furtherance of the computerized approach, I have found that a paper "scanner" is a valuable add-on (approx. $100-$200 cost) because it reduces the overwhelming pile of insurance/hospital/physician correspondence into neat, mobile, organized, secure computer files. This helps in keeping up with the seemingly arbitrary referral/approval requirements, ensures proof of insurance requirement compliance and minimizes the depressing financial after-effects of your hospital stay without disrupting your life. I find the scanner most helpful in organizing submitted claims because insurers, or at least their employees, have a tendency to decline coverage for invalid reasons. They also have a tendency to lose submitted claims. As a result, some patients just assume the service wasn't covered or they lose track of what they submitted, what was covered, what was denied, how much was paid, etc. I just match the insurance company's "Explanation of Benefits" form against my computerized claim copy. If I'm not satisfied, I simply resubmit the claim until I'm convinced my claim was properly evaluated.

Some of this organizational "stuff" might seem like overkill but it will prepare you for your almost certain battle with your insurer and will save you hours of frustration, potentially thousands of dollars, and, most importantly, will speed your recovery (or at least not slow it down). Often my friends ask me how to deal with the barrage of bills, forms and declination letters (i.e. "We regret to inform you that the submitted claim for medical services is denied because that service is not covered under your benefits policy") that inevitably follow hospitalizations and medical problems. My simple answer is: "Stay organized and don't take it personally." One friend in particular who had an extremely seriously-ill newborn, and never had the time to get or stay organized due to the sudden circumstances thrust upon her, finds the aftermath process to be one that is insensitive, illogical, never-ending and depressing.

However, once I explained to her that she shouldn't take it personal and that her efforts will result in money-saved by her family, she looks at it as a job she has inherited along with a now healthy son.

WILLS, LIVING WILLS AND POWERS OF ATTORNEY

In almost all planned hospital admissions, death, disability and being rendered mentally incompetent occur rarely. However, the prospective hospital patient and his/her family should consider these possibilities and, if appropriate, prepare the following three (3) documents prior to hospital admission: 1. Last Will and Testament; 2. Living Will; and 3. Durable Power of Attorney ("POA"). Most people are familiar with the Last Will and Testament as being the legal document by which a person accounts for the disposition of his or her estate and/or personal belongings after death. Depending upon the age, financial circumstances and personal belongings of the individual, this document is not essential for the patient. For example, a child need not have a Last Will and Testament prior to admission unless of course she has the rare rookie Mickey Mantle baseball card in her collection!

The "Living Will," also know as an "Advance Directive" or "Health Care Power of Attorney," is a document by which a competent individual can set forth in advance his/her wishes for health care in the event of subsequent incapacity. Unlike the traditional Will, the Living Will is essential for any living person regardless of their age. Its enforceability is predicated upon statutes in all 50 states enabling individuals to carry out their right to self-determination. To that extent, the Living Will directs when and in what circumstances life-sustaining treatment should be withheld or withdrawn. A slight variation of the

Living Will is the "Health Care Proxy" which is a written document wherein the individual appoints another person as his agent, proxy or health care representative to make medical decisions on his behalf in the event of incapacity. It is more flexible than the Living Will and, because of its more "free-form" nature, can address situations not contemplated in the Living Will.

Mental incompetence, the trigger for the operation of the Living Will, is a legal standard by which a person is determined to not be acclimated to time and place and therefore incapable of providing informed consent. The standard and the proof required, varies from state-to-state. It can be temporary and can often be the result of medication. However, life-saving and/or life-sustaining treatments can unfortunately be required during these periods of incompetence/incapacity. As a result, it is essential that one's wishes be put forth in a Living Will prior to admission to the hospital. Most hospitals require patients to execute uniform or generic Living Wills as part of the admission process. These forms are typically copied from state-enacted statutory forms. However, these uniform/generic forms are extremely basic and do not account for the specific scenarios that could be encountered by senior citizens, children, pregnant women, individuals with unconventional religious beliefs and staunch proponents of alternative medicine. Therefore, either be as specific as possible in your Living Will or grant a Health Care Proxy to a person who is intimately familiar with your wishes and beliefs.

From a practical perspective, young adults would be wise to choose anyone but their parents as the Living Will representative or Health Care Proxy decision-maker because that responsibility might cause unfathomable anguish for a parent or worse, non-compliance with the intended wishes. For example, I know my parents would have a difficult time honoring my Living Will decision to withdraw life-sustaining medical treatment. That is a situation I hope I am never in but it is also one I would never thrust upon my parents. It is also important to choose several alternates in the event the appointed person is unable or unwilling to carry out your wishes. After the document is finalized, bring a copy to the hospital and send one to the physician primarily responsible for your care. Lawyers typically charge approximately $250 for preparation of the Living Will but additional hourly rates may apply for greater specificity and sophistication. For your reference, I have attached a sample Living Will in Appendix A.

Another scenario that often occurs, most frequently with senior citizens, is temporary or permanent physical disability. In this instance, there is no threat for end of life, and the patient retains mental competency but, for whatever reason, the patient is unable to perform various physical tasks. For example, an elderly person might be hospitalized for several months and not be able to attend to paying bills, perform banking tasks, etc. In this instance, it is very important that the individual execute a POA which provides the designated person the power to perform these functions on the patient's behalf. The POAs are drafted many different ways with the safest ones "springing" into effect upon a disability and being fully "revocable" at the end of said disability. Some limit the powers that the POA can accomplish. Others are extremely broad in scope. Lawyers typically charge approximately $300 for the preparation of a POA but again additional hourly rates may apply depending upon the specificity and sophistication required. For your reference, I have attached a sample POA as Appendix B.

When a client, friend or family member lets me know that they will be entering the hospital, I inform them that they should have these three (3) documents in place. Usually they ignore me and thankfully have never had experiences that made them regret that decision. A regrettable decision would be one that forces the patient's family to bear the cost and emotional toll of looking to the judicial system to obtain a guardianship so that their loved one's affairs or medical decisions can be addressed while he or she is physically or mentally incapacitated.

GET YOUR GAME FACE READY

As for the emotional component, the patient must understand that physicians and nurses are merely employees of the hospital or of a practice that has hospital privileges. Accordingly, individual patient problems, requests and situations are run-of-the-mill. While these medical professionals attempt to be sensitive, understanding and compassionate, an integral part of their training is to ensure that their emotions do not affect patient care. In the long run, we as patients benefit from this type of treatment. However, this almost cold attitude could be shocking to patients expecting medical professionals to treat them with the same care and concern as a family member. In a sense, each patient is a number and treated as such. This is not a knock at hospitals or medical professionals - it is just reality. Forget TV shows like "ER," "Chicago Hope," and "L.A. Doctors." Physicians and nurses do care – they just don't, and won't, show it. As you will learn in later chapters, ironically this apparent apathetic behavior is often the key to receiving excellent medical care.

CREATE A SUPPORT SYSTEM

Given the somewhat emotion-less environment, it is therefore important for the patient to set up a "support system" before entering the hospital. Setting up this "support system" requires that each patient inform friends and family of the nature and duration of the hospital stay. This puts friends and family on notice of the impending hardship. Hopefully, they respond and contact you in the hospital. Keep in mind, however, each friend or family member may chose a different approach. Some will visit, others will phone. Some will send flowers/gifts, others will make charitable donations. In any event, particularized interest from friends and family makes the hospital stay more palatable.

This "support system" is very similar to the one that exists between professional sports teams and their fans. Players who play before empty stadiums probably do not have as much adrenaline, and thus as great a drive to succeed, as those players do who play before capacity-packed stadiums. Team executives therefore sell tickets for the sole purpose of creating this "support system" because they know the capacity-packed environment is a vital element to winning. As a patient, the interest and actions of your friends and family provides that winning environment and breaks through the cold, sterile hospital atmosphere. You will find great comfort knowing that people are rooting for you. This is a very powerful phenomenon that is wonderful to experience. Sure, you will have vacant seats (i.e. inconsiderate friends, selfish family members) but the phone calls, visits and flowers will motivate you to recuperation.

BRING YOUR SENSE OF HUMOR

Now, the practical considerations. What should you pack? The most important item for the patient to pack is a sense of humor. So many "things" happen in a hospital that are just beyond a sense of logic or fair play. These occurrences can only be comprehended with a sense of humor. For example, I was once awakened at 2:00 AM by a hospital's television representative to collect $5.00 that was due for a day's service. I was two days post-op from spine fusion surgery and hadn't yet turned the television on. He came into the room, turned on the lights and loudly introduced himself. He said I owed $5.00 for one (1) day's service and asked whether I would be interested in pre-paying for the duration of my hospital stay. I was familiar with hospital policy regarding the charges and as I awakened I remembered having asked my nurse to activate the service but then I suddenly became frightened that my debt was such a high priority!

Once I realized I wasn't on "Candid Camera," I began cursing at the representative. When he came closer toward my bed, I saw he was no more than seventeen years old and by the look on his face he had no idea how inconsiderate and stupid his actions were. I then paid him Twenty ($20) Dollars and warned him to never come into my room after 9:00 PM unless he became a doctor. I then asked if he ever thought about how he might feel if he were so interrupted at 2:00 AM two days after major surgery to pay $5.00 for television service. He just looked at me as if I were speaking a foreign language.

A sense of humor is also required to endure the constant probing of your body and orifices by doctors, interns, residents, fellows, nurses, etc. For example, it is not uncommon in a teaching institution to have the most uncomfortable of examinations performed by three or four different people within minutes of each other. My intimate familiarity with this scenario was a motivating image behind writing this book. In one instance, I spooked a young male resident when he came in to perform what would have been my third rectal examination by a different physician within an hour of one another. As he professionally introduced himself and proceeded to patronize me with his apparent understanding of my dignity concerns, I interrupted him. Then, with a straight face, I said, "I don't mean to rush you but I'm really looking forward to my rectal exam - do you think we can do that now and resume talking later?" His startled facial expression was priceless. He then tried to compose himself, looked down at my medical records and in a surprised but professional tone came to the conclusion that the exam wouldn't be necessary after-all since I had one fifteen (15) minutes prior to his arrival. Needless to say, I wasn't bothered anymore during that hospital stay for that particular examination.

It is also not uncommon to endure patient history questions from the same individuals within minutes or hours of each other. Sometimes you are in such severe pain or in such dire need to rest it is totally unreasonable to comply with the second, third and fourth requests to yet again have an orifice probed or your history questioned. However, you have to understand that this is how these medical professionals hone their skills. It gets incredibly frustrating but you must understand this is being done for your benefit and for the benefit of patients that follow you. Just laugh. On the other hand, if your normal daily routine includes having the various orifices of your body probed repeatedly by different people within minutes or hours of each other or if you are a hypochondriac, you will not have a problem in this area.

What about what not to bring? Do not bring your need for total privacy because it will be violated almost immediately upon your arrival. Again, this is not a criticism of hospitals or medical professionals. This "violation" is necessary to obtain treatment. You will also need to leave home some of your dignity requirements. To that extent, try to understand that often you will not have control over how, when or by whom you are treated. Hospital workers are professionals and will appreciate your understanding because they are also human and therefore uncomfortable about some of the things they must do, as well as, how and when they must do them. As a result, they will do all they can to respect your privacy and dignity rights. Keep in mind, however, it is virtually impossible to completely honor individual privacy and dignity requirements.

PACKING THE ESSENTIALS

In order to function on a day-to-day basis, you need to bring certain items to the hospital. You should bring these items in a "carry-on" type piece of luggage that has several easy access compartments. Do not bring your best luggage - just bring something that is easily portable and functional. The items you need to bring include, but are not limited to, clothes, bathroom accessories, personal effects, etc. Set forth below are some that I recommend:

- **Clothes**: Bring comfortable clothes but those that can withstand being damaged in the event they are stained or soiled with blood or other bodily fluids. You do not need to bring a change of clothes for every day because the first few days you will probably be dressed in a hospital gown or pants. However, undergarments for each day are necessary so that you can maintain some sense of control over your cleanliness, dignity and privacy. The type of surgery or tests you are having will dictate the type of clothes but you can't go wrong with sweat apparel. I usually bring several pair of sweat pants and sweatshirts. I also bring several old T-shirts and several pairs of socks. The sweatshirts are important because your body temperature gets completely thrown off by the surgery and/or the medications you receive prior to or after the surgery. For example, after the intravenous pain medication is discontinued, my body frequently experiences deep chills (commonly referred to as "Goose Fever") for several days. At the same time, I also seem to sweat profusely. The only thing that keeps me comfortable are layered sweatshirts. As you might have intravenous lines running into your arms it's usually best to bring zippered sweat shirts or ones that are cut off on one of the arms to provide the nurse with easy intravenous access.

- **Slippers**: In real life, I do not wear slippers. However, in a hospital they are an absolute must since the "slippers" supplied by the hospital are usually no more than paper mache or cheap "airline" socks. Since you will be required to walk around as part of your recuperation, slippers will protect you from coming in contact with another patient's bodily fluids or other foreign materials. I also find slippers to be comforting from a psychological perspective because they seem to separate my body from the hospital floor. The slippers I usually wear are those that once belonged to my father who has endured more than his share of hospitalizations and is the toughest person I know. As a result, these ugly, worn-out slippers are a source of great inner strength.

- **"LifeSaver" Candies**: During many of my hospitalizations I am unable to eat solid food and thus limited to hospital pudding and jello. As prisoners-of-war are given more appetizing options, I live on "LifeSaver" candies. These candies also come in handy for me when I'm not supposed to eat at all because, by definition, consuming them is not technically eating – it is sucking. Being an attorney has its advantages! Seriously, follow your physician's instructions regarding eating restrictions particularly prior to surgery (primarily because of anesthesia ramifications), but I've always considered "LifeSavers" to be a safe way to cheat, and thus survive, after surgery.

- **Bathroom Accessories**: The hospital provides you with very generic supplies such as shampoos and soaps but I always find it important to bring my own "stuff." Whether it's the smell of my shampoo or the feel of my razor, this gives me back some control over my personal appearance despite the catheters and tubes sticking out of my body. Besides, I always find it somewhat discomforting that after bathing with the hospital's "stuff," I still smell exactly the same as the 95 year-old female patient two doors down the hall. Other items to consider are nail-clippers, Q-tips, powder and deodorant. It is also important to bring your own "stuff" because managed care cost constraints are resulting in less and less complimentary accessories. In fact, your nurse may be more than willing to provide you with another water basin or shampoo container but he or she may enter this request in the hospital computer as an additional charge. You might also consider bringing ear plugs or the airplane-issued type eye patches. Between the interruptions from the nurses, doctors, diligent television representatives, the hospital's strange schedule and perhaps the habits of your roommate (i.e. snoring, all-night television/reading), these items could be essential in helping you rest. While I would not classify "nose-plugs" as necessities, they have helped me combat the "trumpet playing" of some gaseous roommates.

- **Telephone Numbers/Addresses**: Do not bring your address book or electronic organizer because you will lose it. However, do bring the numbers of the people you think you'll need or want to contact.

- **Writing Materials**: Bring enough writing materials to jot down notes in the event you need to make a list of questions for your doctors or if you need to communicate in writing because you will not be able to speak after your surgery or test.

- **Medications**: If you are on medications at home for conditions unrelated to your hospital stay, give them to the nursing staff. Since the advent of managed care, I have found that hospitals occasionally charge more for prescription drugs than retail pharmacies. I have also found that insurance companies reimburse less for hospital-dispensed medications than they do for those purchased from a drug store. This is not a critique of hospital or insurance company policies. It is simply a potential loophole in managed care prescription drug reimbursement. In any event, when you bring medication to the hospital, it is essential that you notify your physician and arrange for its proper administration.

- **Eyeglass Cases**: My eyeglasses were once inadvertently knocked off my bedside table while a nurses' aid recklessly made my bed. The lenses fell out of the frames that incidentally had split in two. The aid just calmly picked up the pieces and delicately placed them back on the table. She then declared that she "thought" my eyeglasses were broken. I "thought" she was a moron! Do yourself a favor and bring an eyeglass case.

- **Reading/Entertainment Materials**: Purchase books and magazines before you go into the hospital. Because I am hospitalized so frequently, I keep a pile of magazines and occupational reading materials that I never get the opportunity to read. I bring this pile to the hospital and catch up. Hopefully, your situation is different and you can simply take the opportunity to read a book you have always wanted to read. I also usually bring an inexpensive radio and headphones (it minimizes any inconveniences to roommates or other patients) so that I can change my entertainment source when it becomes stale.

- **Valuables**: You will need to bring some money to the hospital to pay for the television service, telephone service, newspapers and other incidentals. While each hospital usually provides for safekeeping of money and other valuables, you would once again be relinquishing control. Therefore, I hold my own money but bring only approximately Sixty ($60) Dollars. Other than an inexpensive watch, I do not bring any other valuables and I advise you to do likewise.

- **Identification**: Bring your Health Insurance Identification Card because upon your admission it might be required. However, do not bring your wallet or credit cards because they will do you no good in the hospital and can only be lost. Sorry to all you late-night television purchasers. It may slice, dice, get you into shape or predict your future, but in the long run it's not worth it.

Now, some miscellaneous preparation issues. In the event you have a condition that causes unexpected hospital stays, prepare a spare packed suitcase and tell a reliable person where it is located. Provide that person with a set of spare keys to your dwelling if it is located at your home, or give them the spare suitcase. This way your hospitalization will cause only minor inconveniences to your friends and family. Additionally, depending upon the duration of your stay, consider shaving any hair off your arms to minimize the discomfort from the intravenous "adhesives" (i.e. the tape used to secure the intravenous lines to your arm). Being "stuck" several times hurts but we all know the worst pain occurs when the nurse rips the tape off. Most nurses understand this universal sensitivity. However, be prepared for the worst possible scenario. To that extent, pre-admission shaving is necessary because the nonchalant, almost condescending, manner in which the nurse pulls the tape off, full-well knowing the pain it inflicts, is mentally infuriating. While the adhesive remnants are easily removed with alcohol, you will enjoy the cleansing process significantly more without the presence of hair.

Chapter 2

A TYPICAL DAY IN THE HOSPITAL: WELCOME TO CLUB MED?

Adjusting to Hospital Routine, Schedule and Atmosphere

I have read the brochures and watched the commercials - - - skiing, snorkeling, golf, scuba diving, fine foods and interesting people. The place where there are no clocks, watches and time schedules. Club Med - - - the antidote to civilization. Let's see - - - cleansing enemas, stimulating occupational therapy, thorough sponge baths, gross food and moody nurses? Okay, the experiences might be somewhat similar in their respective offerings of diverse activities, but unlike a Club Med vacation, routine, schedule and a sterile atmosphere drive the hospital stay. Continuing to function as an individual within these parameters is important in successfully coping with the hospital's psychological and physical restraints. This chapter details the routine, schedule and atmosphere.

Except for patients admitted strictly for medical purposes, the hospital patient experience primarily begins after surgery, when you are transported to a "Recovery Area" for several hours or days depending upon your condition. This is a room or large sterile area equipped with sophisticated monitors and staffed with nurses specifically trained in general post-op treatments. After you are stabilized, you will be transported to a floor "most suitable" to the care requirements of the particular type of surgery or procedure you underwent. "Most suitable" because bed availability could have an effect. You will eventually, however, be placed on a floor where the nurses are trained to treat your specific condition. Thereafter, surgical and medical patients experience similar schedules.

Once situated on a floor, the defining time periods of your day essentially revolve around physician visits, medication time intervals and meals. These are the basic parameters but you could also be interrupted during the day for various diagnostic tests, blood taking, re-insertion of intravenous needles and if you are fortunate, visits from friends and family. You can also expect to be visited by an appropriate member of the hospital's clergy and a hospital staff nutritionist. I prefer to be visited by the clergy first so I can then pray for a pretty nutritionist.

"INTERNS,"
"RESIDENTS" AND "ATTENDINGS"

What about the actual difference between these physician designations? Generally, the medical students you encounter are in their third and fourth years of school. During this period they function primarily as professional rectal examiners, history-takers and "Attending" ass-kissers. After their fourth year, they embark upon a three-year residency in a specific area of medicine. In the first year of residency, they are commonly referred to as "interns" which they immediately discover is the Latin word for "schmuck" because they are incredibly overworked by more senior residents who function as the day-to-day bosses and "Gods-in-training." During the second and third years of residency, interns are formerly referred to as "residents." After residency, a physician becomes an "attending" to denote that he or she is a real doctor finished with training. Attendings are medically and legally responsible for the hospital patient. If you are admitted to the hospital for surgery, typically your surgeon is the attending physician.

Some physicians desire bigger houses and faster cars so they strive to become "specialists." This involves at least a two-year specialization after residency commonly referred to as a "fellowship." It also eventually requires the passing of a specialty certification exam. While they are in the fellowship program they are referred to as "fellows." After passing the certification exam they are full-fledged specialists such as gastroenterologists, cardiologists, urologists, etc. and therefore qualified to dump the spouse who stuck by them in the smaller house and slower car.

<u>"ROUNDS"</u>

Surgeons, specialists and attendings make their "rounds" at approximately 6:30 AM to 7:00 AM. The term "rounds" refers to the process by which physicians visit each of their patients to check on status. Usually medical "students," "interns," "residents" and/or "fellows" accompany your surgeon or attending. You can usually figure out a physician's place in this medical "hierarchy" from your initial interaction with the particular physician. For example, students, interns and residents will spend much more time with you than surgeons and specialists. However, most of that time will be spent with their fingers up your behind performing rectal examinations. To that extent, you need to identify them beforehand so you can turn the other cheek or boast of your unbridled anticipation of the rectal exam.

Once you familiarize yourself with the timing of the rounds, make sure you are alert during that time period. This enables physicians to best assess your condition and affords you the opportunity to effectively pick their brains. Unfortunately, you will likely be fast asleep when they arrive and then be suddenly awakened by the intimidating presence of several physicians hovering over your bed. The "chief" or physician in charge will then literally quiz the underlings (i.e. interns, residents, and fellows) about your symptoms, treatment and prognosis. As you undoubtedly will have established a trusting relationship with some of the underlings in the course of your hospital stay, you have a rooting interest in their answers because it is not comforting to find out that he or she is a moron! Still, with all this going on, you must be candid in answering their questions and assertive in asking yours.

Both the surgeon and specialist may visit you but each visit will be separate. Surgeons, in my experience, arrive closer towards 6:30 AM while specialists make their rounds more towards 8:00AM. Depending upon your condition, your doctors may make rounds twice in the day with the second visit occurring in the early- to late- afternoon. Rest assured, however, interns, residents and fellows are readily available during the day should you encounter a problem. Nurses can also immediately contact your surgeon or specialist. While you are under the care of a surgeon, it is usually unnecessary for your specialist to have a "hands-on" approach since all your needs are being taken care of by the surgeon. However, I have found that because of the complications of my Crohn's Disease, I rely on my specialist to prescribe medications and keep an eye on the bigger picture, that is, my overall health. You should discuss this with your physician before you enter the hospital because some, by default, may not begin treating you until you are out of the care of the surgeon.

PAIN MANAGEMENT

You may also be visited during this time period (as well as at various other times of the day) by the "Pain Management Team." These are anesthesiologists specifically trained to treat your post-op or other pain. Anesthesiologist have always perplexed me because they do not solicit patients and are thus not specifically selected by patients. They just pick up their patient assignments and "knock em' out" before surgery. Since most of their patient interaction occurs while patients are unconscious, I always thought they must have been the shyest medical students or the ones with the worst personalities. After interacting with Pain Management Teams over the years I realized this wasn't true – those students become radiologists! Seriously, you will find the pain management physicians to be the most personable of the physicians. However, some surgeons and mainstream specialists look down upon the "pain management" specialty as an unnecessary accommodation to patients. As a result, the Pain Management Team usually visits at offbeat times of the day to minimize any negative physician interactions. Pain will unfortunately be a frequent visitor during your hospital stay and it is your patient right to be as pain-free as is safely possible. Remember that and do not be intimidated by physicians who tell you to simply deal with the "discomfort." "Discomfort" spoken of in normal settings means having to readjust the pillows you're laying on. "Discomfort" out of the mouth of a physician in a hospital setting means: "If that were me I'd be on Demerol, but it's you so just take two Tylenol and stop bothering me!"

BREAKFAST???

Breakfast is usually served between 8:00 AM and 9:00 AM. However, by this time your body has probably been probed and prodded by surgeons, interns, residents and fellows that you have lost your appetite. This is also when the nursing assistants begin making their rounds. In some hospitals these are nursing students and in other hospitals they are merely good-intentioned gofers. In any event, most are qualified to do no more than break your eyeglasses. Their function primarily is to make your bed and bathe you if you are unable or unwilling to do so. Often they arrive earlier but I suggest putting them off until after breakfast so you don't miss impromptu visits by doctors. I say this because when physicians see that you are in the middle of being bathed they will usually just come back "later." However, "later" is unpredictable. Worse, they might examine you while you are in the middle of being bathed. An examination under such circumstances is unfair to the physician, patient and nursing assistant. Accordingly, put everything off until after you have seen your physician. This will also help create some form of order to your day.

Between 9:00 AM and 10:00 AM there is usually a senior citizen volunteer slowly walking around the floors selling newspapers or pushing a library cart. If you want a newspaper every day, ask your morning nurse what time this occurs. Then inform the seller of your wishes. They usually do not have the tenacity of the television representatives and will let you slide if you can't muster up the $.35 or if you aren't in the room when they stop by. As you may be taken out of the room for diagnostic tests, it is important to develop a good rapport with the seller so your newspaper is on your meal tray when you return.

ROUTINE NURSING VISITS

In addition to the events mentioned above, your nurse comes by every few hours to medicate you. Additionally, nurses or nursing students/interns annoyingly check your vital signs (i.e. blood pressure, pulse and temperature) on almost an hourly basis and they do so with the same urgency as a surgeon attempting to clamp off your aorta! Nurses also stop by when they come on shift to evaluate your condition and assess your care requirements. This gives them an idea as to the amount of attention you might require during that particular shift. This is important to nurses because they are extremely short-staffed each sometimes being responsible for anywhere between eight and thirteen patients. Any assistance your condition can offer in terms of prioritizing their efforts is worthwhile. A more detailed description of nursing care is provided in Chapter 3.

In the mid- to late- morning, after you have bathed, it is usually time to get up and, depending upon your condition, walk or participate in physical/occupational therapy. When you are not mobile, usually you are fitted with a pressure-induced "sock" that periodically stimulates the blood flow in your feet and legs. This is done to lessen the chance of blood clots, bedsores or other damage that may be caused by immobility. If you've ever put a quarter into a motel vibrating bed, you can imagine how annoying these "socks" can be.

<u>LUNCH</u>

Lunchtime, 11:30 AM to 12:30 PM, usually brings peace. You can enjoy lunch because physicians are usually not around. After lunch, unless you are transported to radiology for diagnostic testing, you have several hours of "down-time" where nothing much is scheduled. This is when you need to entertain yourself with television, radio, magazines, etc. As I have never been one for daytime television, one way I have kept my sanity during the down-time is by listening to SportsTalk radio shows like WFAN's "Mike and The Mad Dog." Proof of my sanity is that despite my numerous hospitalizations I have never called in to their show! Nevertheless, it is during this downtime when I most often become depressed. I suspect this is similar for other patients. As such, this is a good time to use the telephone. Phone calls received during this downtime always mean a great deal to me because they make the day fly by.

MAKING FRIENDS

I also recommend trying to get to know your roommate during the downtime. Who knows, you might make a friend, gain a client, begin a business relationship, etc. I also try to take this opportunity to find children on the floor faced with problems with which I am familiar. While my health problems have caused me great difficulty, I suppose it would have been a far greater hardship if I were diagnosed with Crohn's Disease as a child. To that extent, I try to find children on the floor, introduce myself and offer my assistance in terms of explaining what they could expect, what they are going through or just to keep their spirits up. I'm not sure my visits help them but they always make me feel better. Sleeping is also an option during the downtime but it is often difficult because the hospital room is bright, telephones are ringing and nurses are constantly walking in and out of the room dispensing medications and checking on your intravenous connections and vital signs.

SECOND ROUNDS

In the late afternoon you may be visited by your doctors making their second rounds. Again, depending upon your condition, this will vary. However, your condition is not the only factor that determines when or how frequent your physician visits. Sometimes it depends upon the physician. I say this because of an experience I had with a physician in Boston. I was hospitalized for a flairup of my Crohn's Disease and put on intravenous medication. However, the doctors were stumped by the severity of my pain. My gastroentorologist at the time, Dr. Peter Banks, was relentless in his pursuit of an answer. I usually saw him in the morning and afternoon. This one particular day, despite his usual diligent efforts, my condition worsened and his afternoon visit left us both feeling confused, defeated and depressed. It didn't help that the diagnostic tests continued to be unsuccessful in pinpointing the problem. That night, however, much to my amazement, at approximately 11:30 PM, Dr. Banks walked into my room in street clothes looking like he had just experienced a brainstorm. He personally wheeled me down to the radiology department, performed some unconventional x-ray and found the answer. The next day I had surgery to fix the problem and was released shortly thereafter. I will never forget Dr. Banks' dedication, determination and conscientious efforts on my behalf. Therefore, while I have set forth the general schedule of physicians, you never know when they may show up. Dr. Banks made me miss the "Tom Snyder" television show that night, but I forgave him.

THE LATE AFTERNOON

For surgical patients, the late afternoon, or down-time, is also a very interesting time of the day as I was to learn during my first "bowel resection" operation in 1986. As general anesthesia causes the intestines and bladder to "sleep," it is important to make sure after the surgery that patients are not permitted to eat or drink until their bowels have awakened. Usually, this requires the presence of bowel sounds to be readily apparent. Physicians typically measure bowel sounds through a stethoscope. However, the expulsion of gas will also suffice. Once this occurs, the patient is permitted to eat/drink. For abdominal surgery patients, however, the scrutiny is much more intense. More specifically, the rules are different because every effort is taken to ensure that not only the bowel has awakened but also that the surgery was successful and all the reattached parts work properly. To that extent, these patients are prohibited from eating solid foods until after they have a bowel movement and can certify same! Furthermore, these patients must then be closely "monitored" after a few days of eating solid foods to ensure the surgery's success. The "monitoring" process consists of bowel movement descriptions regarding odors, textures, density and size. There is nothing like being a grown man and summoning a nurse into the bathroom to evaluate your latest accomplishment. As a result, sometimes my sole aspiration in the hospital is to flush without permission.

With so much riding on the passing of gas, it is not uncommon to tighten up like a basketball player missing a decisive free throw before a hostile crowd with three seconds left in the game. You've done it thousands of times all alone in the gym, in college and even in your backyard, but now all of a sudden at this moment you feel as if you will never fart again! As I was to find out, desperate times made for desperate measures.

During that 1986 surgery I had not expelled gas for several days and was being tortured because other patients were eating and I could not. During the down-time, some of the other less-fortunate patients and I walked the hallways specifically trying to stimulate the expulsion of gas. With our rear ends stuck out and knees bent, we were fixated on trying to hit that "free throw!" If that wasn't bad enough, our objective and its associated frustrations became the primary topic of conversation between us, our families and friends. After a while my friends/family were reluctant to visit because they couldn't stand the gaseous focus.

After passing gas and holding down liquids, the next frustration was the bowel movement. You'd think that one would naturally follow the other but just as good free throw shooters can't always shoot from the corner – there were some problems. Again, during the down-time patients tried to somehow effectuate this natural phenomenon. To make matters worse, during that particular hospital stay there were no bathrooms in the patient rooms. Instead, there were two co-ed bathrooms in the hallway. As a result, there were literally lines of enthusiastic patients outside the hallway bathrooms hoping that when they got their opportunity they would make a splash! I had a roommate who was so frustrated by his inability to perform these functions that he became emotionally disturbed. The physicians put him on tranquilizers to calm him down so that his thoughts were not focused on whether or not he expelled gas and thus graduated to the bowel movement level.

<u>DINNER</u>

Between 5:15 PM and 6:15 PM, dinner is usually served. This is usually a peaceful time. After dinner, if you are fortunate, visitors begin to arrive. Friends and family also begin to telephone after dinnertime. It is important to note that hospitals set up the phone systems so that patients cannot receive incoming calls past a certain time. This is done so as to not disturb patients seeking rest. The "shut-down" time varies depending upon the hospital. I have experienced it as early as 9:00 PM and as late as 11:00 PM. So if your phone does not ring after 9:00 PM, don't think it's because no one is thinking about you.

Between 7:00 PM and 9:00 PM you are pretty much left alone because the hospital recognizes this as the visitation period. If you ever went to sleep-a-way camp, this is analogous to "Elective Hour." However, there will be some nights your roommate has visitors and you do not. This can be a source of great anxiety but you must understand this happens to every patient. You also must be understanding if your roommate has several visitors and these visitors are loud or they tend to crowd the room. Your first inclination may be to tell everyone to quiet down and leave the room but don't forget that the next night the situation could be reversed.

THE LATE SHIFT

After 9:00 PM nurses tend to visit patients a bit more frequently to get a handle on conditions and prepare for bedtime. If they could, I think nurses would put patients to sleep at 9:00 PM to minimize their night shift difficulties but most patients try going to sleep at 11:00 PM. Given that your day essentially starts at 6:30 AM, it is prudent to try to get to sleep as early as possible. However, I usually have difficulty following this suggested bedtime because I need a couple of hours to contemplate thoughts, ideas and other things that I never get a chance to think about during the hectic pace of my life. Therefore, I usually forego sleeping medication until later on after I have had an opportunity to relax. Besides, it is only at this time when you can watch television un-interrupted. For me, this time has usually been between 11:30 PM and 1:30 AM. Thank you Jay Leno, Ted Koppel and Tom Snyder.

Usually after watching Tom Snyder, I summon the nurse and take my sleeping medication. I'm dating myself with the mention of Mr. Snyder because his show went off the air in 1999 but he deserves mention as there was something about that man which soothed my pain and calmed my fears. Thanks to TS, as Mr. Snyder refers to himself, and modern pharmacology, this begins my four to five hours of sleep. However, I am usually interrupted during my sleep by technicians taking blood samples, the TV service collection agency, nursing assistants playing "doctor" or by the beeping sound of the machine which regulates the intravenous medication. When I fall back to sleep I dream of water skiing, snorkeling and golf only to be awakened by several physicians standing over my bed quizzing me about gas, pain, and bowel movements. No, this is not Club Med.

Chapter 3

NURSES

THE GOOD, THE DEDICATED AND THE FOLEY CATHETER

I was awakened from the anesthesia by the incredible pain in my buttocks. I had just undergone spine fusion surgery where a piece of bone from my buttocks was removed and then strategically reinserted to stabilize my back at the "L5-S1" level. Prior to surgery, I was told everything would be held together with "hardware" (i.e. screws, nuts and bolts) to initiate eventual bone fusion. With this in mind, I gingerly tried to shift my body position but my body wouldn't listen. The severity of the pain distracted it from taking orders. I was not in control. I tried to speak but my mouth was covered by an oxygen mask. To make matters worse, the movement of my lips revealed that my teeth were chattering as my body shivered to fight against the effects of the almost sub-arctic temperatures of the operating room.

My mind soon began to clear but the sensations of pain and cold were getting more intense. I had a strong urge to urinate but was distracted by the priorities of pain and warmth. However, nature was calling and I had to pick up the phone. I looked under the sheet down toward my private area and thankfully saw that there was no need to "pick up the phone" for it was busy. A "Foley Catheter" had been inserted into my bladder through my penis so that I would not have to leave the bed to urinate. I thought about the pain, cold and confinement. Then I looked back up at the ceiling and felt as vulnerable as a human being can feel.

As the anesthesia continued to wear off, pain and cold set in for real. It was as if I had awakened from a nightmare only to find out it wasn't a nightmare. Suddenly, the confinement of the narrow bed, the sounds of the monitors and my complete inability to "toss" or "turn," flashed panic signals to my brain. As my eyes focused, I noticed a cord hanging over the bed-rail almost touching my left shoulder. At the end of the cord was a red button. Having had many surgeries, I knew what this button was and I knew I needed to reach for it. I ordered my right hand to move across my body to pull on the cord. I then put my right thumb on the button and pushed. The depression of the button triggered a loud beeping noise clearly distinguishable from the sounds of the various monitors. I had done all I could. Now I just prayed. Within a couple of seconds a nurse came running to my side. She moved the oxygen mask away from my nose and I screamed of my pain and fright of freezing to death. I begged her for blankets and asked her to help me reposition my hips. She calmly assured me I'd be fine and then quickly found several wool heavy blankets and covered me head to toe. She also gave me another dose of pain medication.

As she checked my intravenous lines, she explained that I was in the Recovery Room and should just relax. Within a few minutes the pain medication kicked in and I fell back to sleep. A few hours later, I was once again awoken by the pain. This time, however, it was a different shift and a different nurse. She did exactly as the first nurse and once again I fell back to sleep.

I was eventually moved into a room on a floor for recovering spine surgery patients. My vital signs had *stabilized enough for the transfer but the pain was actually more intense. When I awakened, I was laying directly on my back incision but wondered if the pain would lessen if I were to lie on my left side. I thought of the left side because the surgeon had taken the bone from my right buttocks. Consequently, lying on my right side was not an option. I pressed the call button and within a few minutes my floor nurse appeared. I asked her to help me reposition my body. She explained that an extra "pull" sheet had been placed underneath my body for this particular purpose but that she needed another nurse to hold the sheet at the opposite end so that they could "shimmy" my body to its new position.*

To ensure that I wound up in the middle of the bed, they turned me on my side before they shimmied. I was frightening by my inability to turn my hips even a fraction of an inch to help them. I felt like a refrigerator being pulled across a tile floor on old towels. Immediately after we settled on a position, I experienced a rebound pain and screamed so deeply that my voice instantly became hoarse.

After lying on my left hip for several minutes, I realized that it was even more uncomfortable then lying on my back. I called the nurse again but this time begged her to move me onto my back. Within a couple of minutes she returned with the other nurse and without even a hint of annoyance accommodated my request. Several minutes later I called again because I was thirsty but was unable to reach the cup of orange juice placed on my meal tray. I felt almost abusive asking a human being to help me with such a trivial task but because of my surgery I had no other choice. Once again, the nurse came immediately and very patiently brought the cup to my mouth so that I was able to sip it without spilling any on my bed or myself. These types of requests continued for several days until my body regained its strength and I was able to help myself.

RESPECT YOUR NURSE

This was my most recent surgical experience that took place in January, 1999. However, it's always been the same each time. That is, the constant that stands between sanity and total panic is the unconditional, reliable, professional and genuinely compassionate care of my nurse. Nurses must be special people because they are required to care for people when people are at their worst. They are required to provide highly technical medical care as well as demanding, often demeaning, custodial care yet they must attend to both responsibilities with the same professional approach. This requires professionalism unprecedented in any job or industry. Even more impressive, they must demonstrate this professionalism to patients who often use their illnesses or afflictions as licenses to abandon all notions of human decency. Physicians may give orders but nurses carry them out. For these reasons, I believe nurses are the most integral part of the healthcare industry.

Depending upon the locale, hospital and shift, floor nurses are each responsible for anywhere between four and thirteen patients. As a result, sometimes nurses do not respond immediately when called. Even on a good day, "immediately" is unrealistic – "within a few minutes" is more accurate. However, I have called nurses for medication and been acknowledged but not received the medication for as long as an hour. I like to think that "tardy" nurses are appropriately preoccupied with the prioritized emergencies of other patients. I like to think that "tardy" nurses are victims of impractical patient-nurse ratios. I like to think that nurses are thus trained to prioritize patient care causing delays that are customary. Of course, I also thought O.J. Simpson was going to be found guilty of murder! Let's face it, there are some nurses who just do not like their jobs. These types of nurses make being a patient very difficult.

Just like in any other profession, incompetent or apathetic employees are often the byproduct of being overworked and/or mistreated by their employers and/or customers. I suppose in the hospital it is more of a "chicken & egg" scenario but I do not blame either party. As a patient, it is sometimes so frustrating when nurses are non-responsive or impersonal that it is very difficult not to be short, nasty and demanding. Conversely, I imagine uncooperative, unappreciative, demanding and rude patients fuel great resentment among nurses. As I believe the patient-nurse relationship holds the key to quality healthcare, patients should enter hospitals with tremendous respect for nurses. While you undoubtedly will encounter a seemingly incompetent or uncaring nurse, a polite, considerate and positive attitude might result in better care. Try to give that nurse the benefit of the doubt. After all, you owe him or her at least that given what they are required to do for you.

THE IMPORTANCE OF PHYSICIAN-NURSE-PATIENT COMMUNICATION

Sometimes uncomfortable situations between nurses and patients are caused by communication failures within the healthcare system. Such failures to communicate can be deadly but thankfully they usually only cause delay or inconvenience. In the movie, "Cool Hand Luke," actor Strother Martin, playing a prison warden, tries making an example of Paul Newman by putting him into shackles in front of the other prisoners. Martin's character explains Newman's punishment as the result of a "failure to communicate." Your doctor's failure to communicate orders to your nurse will not cause you a similar fate. Surely, you will not end up in shackles or be compelled, as

Newman's character was, to eat fifty (50) hard boiled eggs in fifty (50) minutes. Your fate could be worse.

MEN: READ THIS

Men, now pay close attention. Three days after I underwent an intestinal resection operation in a suburban Boston hospital, I was resting comfortably in my bed with intravenous lines in my arm, an "NG" (naso-gastric) tube in my nose and a Foley Catheter in my penis. I had already begun to exhibit bowel sounds and was permitted to drink liquids. Consistent with this progress, my surgeon came in during the late afternoon and removed the Foley Catheter. This was not a pleasant experience. However, the prospect of walking without having that prized-part of my anatomy attached to a mechanical apparatus gave me the courage to get through the awkward withdrawing technique. Immediately after the removal, my surgeon and nurse were abruptly summoned to another patient room for an emergency. They forgot to mention that my urine output had to be measured during the next few hours to ensure that my bodily functions were operating properly. More specifically, I was supposed to urinate or "void" into a portable urinal and have the output measured by the nurses. If my output did not reach a certain amount within a few hours, it would be assumed that my internal organs had not "awakened" sufficiently for me to function without the Foley Catheter. If that became the case, for my safety, the Foley Catheter would be reinserted.

As this was the third day after my surgery, I was still in a tremendous amount of pain having had my entire abdomen sliced open. I could barely move on my own but somehow found the strength to make it to the bathroom every time I had to urinate. I suppose that once the Foley Catheter was taken out, my genitals, feeling liberated, were not interested in continued claustrophobic exercises such as urinating into a portable urinal.

So, after the Foley Catheter was removed, I simply urinated into the toilet. After I finished, I flushed. Call me crazy, but that's how my parents trained me.

About seven (7) hours later, at approximately 1:00 AM, a nurse came into my room and woke me up. She began interrogating me about my urine output. I explained that I had been urinating into the toilet and that everything seemed to be fine. She picked up the portable urinal and noted its empty status. I tried to explain the whole "liberation" theory but she wasn't interested. Since there was no measured output, she sternly said she was coming back to reinsert the Foley Catheter. At that point in time, every Foley Catheter I had ever had was inserted during surgery while I was unconscious. The thought of having this device inserted into my bladder through my penis while I was awake had me feeling, well, kind of freakin' terrified! I thought about calling my parents but they were 200 miles away in New Jersey. It also would have scared them to hear from me in such a frightened state. Since I had just moved to Boston to begin law school and had no friends to call (aspiring lawyers don't make friends so fast), I did not know what I was going to do when she returned.

When the nurse returned, she came with Foley Catheter in hand. We argued for several minutes but she insisted that <u>my health</u> and <u>her job</u> were on the line. She pointed out the health risks but focused more on her responsibility to follow protocol. More specifically, the protocol was as follows: no measured output within a few hours of removal required reinsertion of the catheter. If she violated protocol and I was injured, she was sure she would be fired and possibly lose her nursing license. I told her she shouldn't worry so much because if she tried to reinsert the Foley Catheter she would lose her job and license anyway because I would kill her! She then apparently retreated but returned ten (10) minutes later with two NFL linebacker-looking nurses in an attempt to hold me down while they reinserted the catheter. (These linebackers missed their calling - they should have worked for the TV service collection agency.) Despite having exhausted all diplomatic measures, I was about to be catheterized against my will. Chuck Norris would have been proud of the way I karate-kicked my way out of the situation.

The nurses, concerned for their respective well-beings, retreated and let me go Foley Catheter-free until the morning but warned me that if I didn't fill up the portable urinal by morning my surgeon would be forced to reinsert it. I spent the night drinking gallons of water and kept my penis inside the urinal even when I wasn't urinating as protection against a return visit by Butkis and Nitchske! When my surgeon made morning rounds he apologized for his "failure to communicate" and noted my sufficient measured output. Not taking any chances, I asked him for a signed affidavit.

There's a moral to this story. I just barely survived the ramifications of a hospital communications problem. While my actual life was not at stake, life as I knew it would have been over had those nurses been successful in catheterizing me. Despite it being embarrassing, the story is important because it illustrates the possible ramifications of hospital communication problems and the motivations of nurses. My nurse was concerned about two things: my safety and her job. Her concerns were probably not in that order. However, my well being was served nonetheless. She did not like me but she maintained her professionalism throughout the ordeal. Sure, I imagine if she had to reinsert the catheter she would have used the same tender touch as Edward Scissorhands - but she's only human. Keep these things in mind when you interact with nurses. Try to understand their motivations as well as their job requirements. If you comprehend these sometimes conflicting pressures, you are more apt to avoid such a bad experience.

NURSING SHIFTS

In keeping with the theme of understanding nurses, you should know that generally there are three (3) nursing shifts: 7:00 AM to 3:00 PM (Day Shift); 3:00 PM to 11:00 PM (Evening Shift); and 11:00 PM to 7:00 AM (Night Shift). Day Shift nurses are usually responsible for eight to ten patients, Evening nurses handle about ten patients while Night nurses deal with approximately thirteen patients. During the Day shift, where two meals are served, medications delivered and diagnostic tests performed, nurses run around the floor like lunchtime wait staff at a busy city diner. As a result, they usually have three nurses' aids while evening shifts have two and night shifts have one. At the end of a nursing shift, each nurse does a bed-to-bed "report" which involves the departing nurse briefing the new nurse on each patient. This report takes approximately ten to thirty minutes. During this time period it is usually very difficult to get assistance because the nurses say they are busy in, what they refer to as, "Report." Doctors have "Rounds," nurses have "Report."

Usually hospitals have Intravenous and Phlebotomy Teams to start intravenous lines and take blood, respectively. However, financial cutbacks in many hospitals have forced staffing reductions so that nurses are now often responsible for these duties. This puts an extra burden on the nurse and compromises the patient because the well-rounded skills of a nurse often pale by comparison to the Team members with respect to starting difficult intravenous lines (e.g. cancer or elderly patients with hard to find or "blown" veins) and taking blood. Therefore, if an intravenous line is required or blood needs to be drawn, ask if there is a specific Team for this purpose. Unless you enjoy getting bludgeoned to start an intravenous line or appreciate the look of black and blue marks, request these specialists, if they are available.

PRIVATE NURSES

Depending upon your desires, insurance plan or income level, private duty nursing is available. I had private duty nursing during only one of my hospitalizations. It was my first abdominal surgery and my parents were concerned that the nurses were too understaffed to address my concerns. They came to this realization two or three days after my surgery when I was waiting thirty to sixty minutes for my pain medication. However, modern technology has all but alleviated this problem via "PCA" machines. These machines permit a patient to safely self-administer powerful narcotics. (For reference purposes, this is the machine that provided the impetus for actor George Clooney's Dr. Ross character leaving the television show, "ER.") As a result, I have survived without private duty nursing. However, looking back at that hospitalization, I remember how my private nurse also made sure I was clean, comfortable and relaxed. When I needed a pillow to hold against my wound in preparation for a cough, I had it in my hands before I asked for it. When I got depressed and practically frightened from the side-effects of one of my medications, she calmed my fears and held my hand until I fell asleep. These are the types of things hospital nurses do but they are so overstaffed that they rarely get an opportunity to do them.

You might want to consider hiring a private nurse for a variety of reasons including, but not limited to: if your condition is complicated and involves the provision of several medications in specific time intervals; if you require intense physical therapy and/or one-on-one physical stimulation; or if your child or elderly relative is the patient and he or she is anxious about the ordeal. Keep in mind though that insurance companies will only cover the cost of these nurses if your doctor deems their presence "medically necessary." As health insurance companies continually tighten their belts in response to the ever-increasing cost of medical care, this "medically necessary" standard is becoming more difficult to meet. To that extent, having the luxury of a pretty nurse holding your hand might not make the grade! Nevertheless, there are legitimate circumstances in which private nurses are medically necessary. In any case, if you can afford it, particularly if it is for a child or an elderly person, indulge - but do it simply because you can. Don't do it because you think you must. Don't do it because you are afraid the hospital's nursing staff will comprise your care. Because if you keep in mind my suggestions and respect the nurses and their profession, you will be in the hands of the most professional and compassionate individuals of our healthcare system.

Chapter 4

PHYSICIANS

JUST REMEMBER THEY ARE
HUMAN BECAUSE THEY SOMETIMES FORGET

Thank You Letter

Dear Dr._____:

Enclosed is a small token of my appreciation of the efforts you asserted on my behalf during my recent stay at _____Hospital for back surgery. {$50.00 gift certificate to Amazon.com}

Having been a hospital patient more times than I care to remember, I found your dedication to my concerns to be unprecedented. These days, whether warranted by managed care constraints or a by-product of stereotypical arrogance, physicians seem to treat symptoms and illness rather than patients. As a result, individual patient needs are often ignored or left unattended. However, you made sure that my individual needs were immediately addressed and that my subsequent concerns were conscientiously monitored. I commend you for your compassion and professionalism.

As for my present condition, I am recuperating rapidly and, according to my surgeon, doing very well. I am slowly weaning off the medications under the guidance of Dr._____ and should be back at work in the near future.

If I can ever use my professional skills to help you, please do not hesitate to call me. Thanks again.

Sincerely,
Michael A. Weiss

Fighting Back Letter

Dear Dr. _____:

I am sure you do not remember, but I came into your office this past December for a surgical consultation regarding severe and persistent back pain. Prior to the scheduled consultation, I had undergone every imaginable diagnostic test, received numerous epidural and cortisone injections and endured six months of physical therapy. I had also been rushed to _____ Hospital on at least three occasions due to the pain and associated inability to walk. While all conventional diagnostic tests were normal, two discograms revealed severe "degenerative disc disease" at the L5-S1 level. According to my internist and physical rehabilitation physician, I was a clear candidate for surgery based upon the aforementioned unsuccessful treatments and positive discograms.

When we met in your treating room, you did not offer me an appropriate opportunity to explain the foregoing circumstances. You merely looked at the MRI exams and conducted a basic neurological examination. I attempted to concisely summarize the circumstances in consideration of your valuable time. As an attorney, I am clearly capable of doing this. Nevertheless, you barely listened and seemed to only pay attention to the high dosages of pain medication I was taking. As I proceeded to emphasize the futility of the aforementioned treatments and conclusive discogram findings, you began dictating a memo to "your file" indicating that you told me to stop taking these medications. Again, I tried to interrupt you to explain the complexity of my situation but you were too busy apparently covering your behind.

Fighting Back Letter
Page 2

After I begged you several times, you finally looked at the discogram images. More accurately, you held the films up to the light in an extremely disorganized fashion and sneered at their results. As an accomplished physician at a world renowned facility specializing in this technique conducted these discograms, I was amazed at the arrogant manner in which you disregarded their significance. I pleaded for you to listen to my plight, but you were only interested in finishing your dictation, and of all things, scheduling a two-to-three week follow-up examination! I commented that a follow-up examination made no sense since my condition had been worsening for the previous six months and would not improve in a few weeks particularly based upon your recommendation of doing absolutely nothing. However, my words once again fell on deaf ears. I then realized that you were not interested in helping me – a person with a serious medical problem. Rather, you seemed only interested in treating symptoms that presented clear-cut surgical cases. I then politely asked you to place my MRI, x-ray and discogram films back in their respective envelopes in chronological order – the order in which I presented them. You promised you had done so. It wasn't until my next surgical consultation with another physician when I discovered you had placed the films back in random order with no care or concern for sequence and proper interpretation.

Fighting Back Letter
Page 3

Since you were the first surgeon with whom I consulted, I was extremely upset when I left your office. In fact, I was in tears. I was frustrated that you <u>couldn't</u> help me but more importantly I was terrified that you <u>wouldn't</u> help me. I would have certainly respected your surgical opinion had you actually attempted to understand my case but what I found very difficult to digest was your complete arrogance, utter lack of compassion and condescending demeanor. However, my faith in doctors was restored shortly thereafter when I consulted with three other orthopedic surgeons who each treated me with dignity and respect. They also <u>all</u> recommended spine fusion surgery. I selected the one of the three in my health plan. The surgery was performed on _____ __, 1999. While I am sure you could care less, it appears the surgery was successful and my pain is gone.

I am not qualified to criticize your opinion and I'm not writing this letter to tell you, "I told you so." My substantially improved condition after surgery speaks for itself. However, it is my right as a patient and consumer to chastise you for the inhumane manner in which you treated me. To that end, the foregoing account of our encounter shall suffice.

Sincerely,

Michael A. Weiss

Business Letter

Dear Dr._____ :

    This letter is in response to the bill I received dated _____ __, 1999 for the co-payment of Fifteen ($15) Dollars for the _____ __, 1998 date of service. (I believe you also saw me a month or so after that date when I was admitted to _____ Hospital for the same problem.)

    While I sincerely appreciate the fact that you squeezed me into your schedule on _____ __, 1998, subsequent events have convinced me that you were completely wrong in the manner in which you treated me. Therefore, as I would with any service that I am expected to pay for, I am declining to pay the Fifteen ($15) Dollars because you did not provide appropriate services. In simple terms, you did not earn your money. More specifically, as you know, I saw you because I had severe back pain. After the _____ __, 1998 consultation, in which you told me that there was nothing wrong with me, I embarked upon a rigorous physical therapy program but I continued to have this severe pain. Eventually it was recommended that I undergo a "discogram" to determine the extent of what appeared to be "degenerative disc disease." When I was subsequently admitted to _____ Hospital, you performed all the routine diagnostic tests the results of which again confirmed your initial diagnosis that there was nothing wrong with me. I explained to you that the physician at _____Institute, who had been overseeing my physical rehabilitation, suggested that I undergo a discogram to diagnose a disc problem that would not appear in the conventional diagnostic testing that you were performing.

Business Letter
Page 2

Despite my plea and moans of severe pain, you discharged me from the hospital despite no improvement whatsoever in my condition. Since my case was not black and white but was rather of a gray variety, you obviously chose not to attempt to probe deeper and potentially locate and fix my problem. While you and your practice have excellent reputations, in my particular case you clearly dropped the ball.

Shortly after leaving _____ Hospital, I did undergo a discogram which revealed that I had severe degenerative disc disease at the L5-S1 level. Subsequently, on _____ __, 1999, I underwent spine fusion surgery to correct this problem. I am presently recuperating from the surgery and all appears to be successful. As I referred to above, this conclusion reveals that you apparently were incorrect in your diagnosis and treatment of me. I am sure you had my best interests at heart and were attempting to solve my problem but you did not look hard enough to find the answer. In other words, you did not earn your money. Other doctors did. To that extent, I respectfully refuse to pay for the services you rendered to me.

I trust you will understand my position and adjust my account accordingly. However, should you have any questions, please do not hesitate to contact me.

Sincerely,

Michael A. Weiss

I wrote these letters to physicians regarding my recent back surgery. All identifying names have been redacted for privacy purposes. These letters reflect the broad spectrum of hospital physician "types" I have encountered although there are a few more, both good and bad, which I describe later in this chapter. The first time my agent read this manuscript he thought these letters belonged in an appendix and that they should be toned down a bit. While I have implemented many of his constructive comments/suggestions, I strongly disagreed with this one because the letters are real, they were mailed and they are symbolic of the only remaining influence/impact patients have in selecting physicians, obtaining quality care and validating the cost of that care. After all, health care is now strictly a business and some providers, insurance companies and their staffs treat patients with the same patronizing respect afforded pimpled-face high school students purchasing their first stereo system. In such instances, when the playing field is not only uneven but also owned, operated and controlled by the seller, the only consumer leverage is word-of-mouth. To that extent, I suspect every person who reads this chapter can relate to these letters. I just hope you have experienced the tremendous satisfaction I got after I sealed, stamped and dropped these letters in the mailbox.

The Thank You Letter was a pleasure to write though ordinarily not necessary but for the increasing existence of the type of physician who warranted the writing of the Fighting Back Letter. Since I believe that if you complain about bad service you have an obligation to compliment individuals whose efforts exceed acceptable standards, I thought it appropriate to commend this particular physician. By way of background, this doctor is an anesthesiologist who was a member of the Pain Management Team assigned to my recovery. When I was coherent in the Recovery Room, I experienced severe pain despite enormous doses of morphine. This was apparently highly unusual. I tried to explain to the Team that, based upon my many surgical experiences, morphine for some reason never helped alleviate my pain. I also indicated I must have a high tolerance for drugs having been on high dosages of narcotics during the six months leading up to my surgery. For some reason, the doctors thought I was just simply articulating an abnormal sensitivity to pain. I begged, screamed and cried trying to enforce my patient right to be free of unnecessary pain but they ignored me.

Thinking that I was incoherent from the effects of the morphine, the doctors spoke freely about me in my presence not fearing that I would comprehend their conversations. However, I overheard one physician comment that my complaints were no big deal since the pain would naturally subside in five-to-seven days! Feeling like I was in a war, shot and left for dead, I persisted in my coherent but loud pleas for help. Finally, I caught the ear of this anesthesiologist who had just been assigned to the Team and had never examined or met me. When I told him what I overheard and gave a lucid description of my previous experiences with morphine and detailed my pre-surgical narcotics dosages, he immediately took me serious and changed my medication to one that was rarely used in the hospital due to its potency. Within an hour, I was as comfortable as I was supposed to be.

This anesthesiologist followed my case from the Recovery Room to my room on the hospital floor. He checked on me several times a day throughout my entire hospital stay and even designed an after-care plan for me to follow upon discharge. Unfortunately, you will not encounter many physicians like him.

As a rule, surgeons and fellows tend to be more distant, mechanical and arrogant while others are more personable. I imagine surgeons act this way because they must while fellows do so because they can. However, with the advent of managed care and the associated competition for patients, all physicians are now virtually required to be more "patient friendly." Except, of course, those that do not need to build and maintain a patient base such as radiologists and anesthesiologists. The ones unable or unwilling to be "patient friendly" are those typical of the doctor addressed in the Fighting Back Letter. They represent the worst in healthcare – the physicians who treat symptoms not people and only do so when there is nothing to gain but money or further development of their God-like self-image. The Fighting Back Letter accurately captures that physician and no further elaboration is required. As for the circumstances that necessitated my writing of the Business Letter, a little background knowledge on "managed care" is required.

MANAGED CARE - WHAT IS IT?

This book is not intended as a primer for "Managed Care" but that phrase keeps popping up so let me provide a brief definition/explanation. "Managed Care" is a catch-all term describing the present state of the healthcare industry whereby insurance companies actively get involved in both negotiating fees for medical services and setting guidelines for treatment. Instead of paying claims submitted by independent doctors, hospitals or patients, managed care companies employ or have contracts with doctors and hospitals then set policies for what they can and can't do. For instance, managed care companies use an authorization process to limit access to specialists, cut down on self-defined unnecessary procedures, and reduce money spent on prescription drugs. The underlying rationale behind managed care is to keep costs down so that more people can have access to medical services.

By way of example and by no means is this an exhaustive definition, two types of managed care organizations are Preferred Provider Organizations ("PPOs") and Health Maintenance Organizations ("HMOs"). In short, PPOs negotiate with medical providers to reduce their charges and the providers in turn are referred business from the PPO. The doctors accept lower fees and agree to controls on their work in exchange for increased patient volume. PPOs often negotiate provider fee reductions in excess of 25%. By contrast, an HMO is a type of health insurance whereby the insurer, rather than the independent physician, provides the health care for a prepaid monthly premium. The HMO doctors are paid a fixed amount per patient (this is called "capitation") regardless of whether a patient is healthy or sick. Thus, while the emphasis is supposedly on "preventative medicine," these physicians have incentive not to do unnecessary surgeries, laboratory or diagnostic tests because often their salaries are adjusted based on how effectively they keep costs down.

In order to go to a specialist (e.g. urologist), a patient in an HMO must go to his/her primary care provider (sometimes referred to as the "gatekeeper") to get a referral. When you don't know what's wrong with you, the system works well. However, when you have a chronic problem for which a specialist normally treats you or if your problem is easily identifiable but nevertheless must be treated by a specialist, the process is comical because you are forced to pay a token visit to the gatekeeper. As I have experienced many recurring chronic problems from having Crohn's Disease, I put my gatekeeper on notice early on that I will not pay such token visits. Instead, I end up explaining my symptoms to his secretary/office manager who then pleads with him to simply issue me the referral. The result is efficient but often embarrassing because I have to disclose my medical problems over the telephone to the secretary/office manager who is a contemporary of mine. It's even worse when several different problems occur within days of each other. Just imagine calling your doctor's secretary on Monday telling her that your prostate is inflamed and you need to see a urologist and then on Wednesday you have to call her again when your hemmorids are acting up and you need a referral to a proctologist!

Some of these managed care plans have financial incentives or rewards for keeping referrals to a minimum or punishments for too many referrals. This sometimes puts some HMO primary care providers in situations where they are encouraged to manage medical conditions that may be beyond the scope of their general training. At least in my case I know before I call that my doctor's secretary is practicing in uncharted territory! As mentioned previously, the upside to these types of managed care plans are cost and accessibility but the downsides include limitations on the choice of physician, choice of facility, duration of hospital stays and types or amounts of drugs prescribed.

A TYPICAL
MANAGED CARE PHYSICIAN

Managed care requires all physicians to exercise business savvy so I am not offended by such actions. However, what HMOs and PPOs are beginning to discover is that patients are entitled to analogous consumer expectations. I tried to convey this in the Business Letter although I did not specify what I really thought happened. More specifically, I thought there was a possibility that this physician wouldn't perform a discogram because my insurance company would not either authorize it or sufficiently reimburse its cost. Moreover, because all conventional diagnostic testing up until that point was negative, I suspected this physician thought the discogram outcome would also be negative and he would therefore have performed a test that wasn't financially "justified." In this case, in order to be financially justified, the results would have to indicate surgery and thus income for him. Having the benefit of hindsight, it is clear that this physician substituted his own prediction of the discogram results at the expense of my welfare simply to avoid the internal financial consequences of performing a negative diagnostic test.

As stated in the Business Letter, another physician had recommended the discogram, but as I was to find out after the fact, my insurance company would only permit my undergoing a discogram if one or more of the other less expensive diagnostic tests were positive. My insurance company's logic was flawed, as you will see in Chapter 9 in which I detail my successful appeal of its denial for the cost of the two discograms I subsequently underwent, because the discogram is designed to diagnose disc problems when all other tests do not. These managed care controlled physicians are the norm nowadays but they can be dealt with so long as you enforce your consumer rights. I never received another bill from this physician and hopefully my successful appeal and arbitration against my managed care company for the cost of the two subsequent "out-of-network" discograms will help other patients in similar predicaments.

TELL THEM WHERE IT HURTS

Doctors are in the business of treating patients, but they can only do so if they are fully informed. Therefore, it is essential that you be completely honest about your symptoms, medications, complaints and concerns. To that extent, write down these items precisely. Conversely, while you must be completely candid with your doctor, your doctor must thoroughly address each and every one of your concerns because you have a right to be fully informed. This interaction is more efficient when you write down your questions in preparation for hospital rounds. Your rights notwithstanding, the reality is that consideration of a physician's time yields more attention and better care.

ASK QUESTIONS

Prior to surgery, some of the information you should inquire about is who will be performing the surgery, what type of technique(s) will be used, are there other options, will there be pain after the surgery and how long is the recuperation process - both in and out of the hospital. After surgery your "right" to be fully informed becomes more of a patient "responsibility" because your care will be delegated from your physician to other hospital staff members. Since the communication chain often breaks down, you need to participate and ask questions to stay informed. If you can't because of the effects of medication or choose not to, delegate the responsibilities to a family member or friend.

Your post-op responsibility to be informed begins when your doctor makes rounds in the morning. Be prepared to ask questions about medications, dosage, eating, discharge date and level of activity. Write down the medication names and dosages. While nurses are extremely dependable, sometimes they make mistakes. As a result, always ask what they are giving you beforehand. If you are having problems sleeping (and everyone does in a hospital) address this with the doctor so that he or she can prescribe sleeping medication. I always ask for sleeping medication just in case because I do not want my nurse to bother either my doctor or the covering physician at 2:00 AM. Do whatever you can to be considerate of your doctor's time. In the hospital this means succinctly addressing your concerns during rounds. If you plan ahead and make your requests in a considerate manner, you will receive quality, compassionate care from your physician.

DEALING WITH PAIN

I have found that one of the most important issues to address with a doctor is pain level. If you are uncomfortable, mention it. Pain medication ("Pain Meds") has significant side effects and addictive ramifications but while you are in the hospital be as comfortable as possible. Don't worry about these ramifications until you are discharged. In the event your physician changes your dosage, make sure that the change is noted in your chart at the nurses' station. If your physician does not discuss the Pain Meds, at least confirm that the dosages are not changing. This is important because some physicians take it upon themselves to lower the dosage if you are not writhing in pain during rounds. Nothing bothers me more than a physician who takes this upon him or herself.

Physicians like to get patients off of Pain Meds as soon as possible because of their detrimental long-term effects but they cannot do so until after consulting with the patient. Just because you are not screaming in pain during the examination does not mean that you are not experiencing severe pain. Some patients, however, think that by confirming the dosage of their Pain Meds they will be looked upon as a drug addict. Given the chaos that often occurs in the hospital setting and the inherent lack of communication in the hospital's bureaucratic design, such confirmation is conscientious and smart. After all, there is no worse feeling in a hospital than being promised certain doses of Pain Meds only to be awakened at 4:00 AM by severe pain and the nurse brings you an aspirin. This is not the nurse's fault - it is the doctor's fault or maybe even your fault for not asserting your right to be reasonably free of pain.

GET TO KNOW YOUR PHYSICIAN TEAM

Before you enter the hospital you deal with only your particular physician and most likely have not even met his or her partners or associates. When you are in the hospital, however, this will be different because your doctor, just like you, takes certain days off. To that extent, if you are in the hospital over the weekend it is likely that an associate or partner will be covering. If this is a sensitive issue to you, it might be a good idea to meet these other physicians before you enter the hospital. Not that you can change your physician's affiliations, but the familiarity might improve your comfort level.

BEDSIDE MANNER OF COVERING PHYSICIANS

Bedside manner is so important in easing my mind, and thus improving my condition, that some of these "covering" physicians have actually detrimentally affected my recuperation. More specifically, I have had experiences where weekend doctors came into my room and simply left after reviewing the clipboard attached to the bed that measured my inputs, outputs and vital signs over various time intervals. Other times, I have asked questions only to be provided with simple yes or no answers in the most condescending of fashions. In my case this has been the rule rather than the exception because I am particularly demanding about bedside manner. However, as they say, "your mileage will vary."

One particular situation, however, was not the covering physician's fault. It was due to the behavior of my parents. It was a snowy Saturday in New York and I was recovering from abdominal surgery in a large New York City hospital located in a part of Manhattan where metered parking was practically impossible and garaged parking cost a small fortune. My parents showed up later than promised and were clearly agitated. It seemed they had a verbal altercation outside the hospital about a prized metered parking spot. My father, who sometimes makes Archie Bunker seem timid, was still seething over what he perceived to be the arrogance of the "SOB" who stole his spot. While I had no mind for the particulars, I felt bad for the other driver because lord knows what my father said to him. Several minutes later in walked the weekend covering physician. Yep, it was the SOB. While they were civil to each other, there was appreciable tension in the air. However, in fairness to the physician, he maintained his professionalism. In fact, he was so thorough that when he gave me a rectal examination I think his finger actually pierced my tonsils!

BEDSIDE MANNER – PARENTS TAKE NOTE

Two educational instances regarding bedside manner stand out in my mind and both occurred the first time I was hospitalized and diagnosed with Crohn's Disease. Prior to my admission to the hospital, I had classic symptoms of what we didn't know then but what turned out to be Crohn's Disease. The symptoms included abdominal cramps, diarrhea, serious digestive problems with fibrous foods, joint pain, fever and a constant lethargic feeling. My family doctor at the time suggested that I seek psychological counseling under the guise that my symptoms were due to anxiety or that I was somehow psychologically causing my own problems. This, by the way, is the typical reaction of some general practitioners to what often turn out to be serious abdominal problems such as Crohn's

Disease. I went along with his suggestion and began treatment with a local psychologist.

The psychologist was very kind and almost "grandfatherly" in his approach but it was clear he felt my problems were directly related to his specialty. Perhaps he was substantiating his own existence as a psychologist but I didn't appreciate his complete disregard for my physical complaints. However, psychological counseling was new to me so I ignored my suspicions of manipulation and kept an open mind. Despite my diligent completion of the ridiculous mental exercises he gave me to perform as homework, several weeks after commencing treatment I was rushed by ambulance to a local hospital with an intestinal obstruction caused by eating popcorn. The pain, which I'm told is comparable to child-bearing labor pains, was so completely unbearable that I thought I was going to die.

I guess I lost complete faith in the psychologist in the ambulance when I overheard the driver tell the hospital that he suspected an intestinal perforation and that they should be prepared to perform immediate surgery to save my life. Up until that point I was trying to perform the mental exercises he had given me to control my anxiety. However, envisioning myself as a "dog in a lounge chair sipping a Pina Colada" seemed like complete quackery at the time! Luckily, I didn't require surgery but was hospitalized for approximately ten days. After a few days when the pain subsided and I was able to safely drink liquids, I had an "Upper GI" and "Barium" series of x-rays that revealed a clear and classic case of Crohn's Disease. After the diagnosis, the hospital's gastroenterologist, who I will blast below, gave me a pamphlet published by the Crohn's & Colitis Foundation of America ("CCFA") which in plain English detailed all the manifestations of the disease as well as the foods that typically triggered flare-ups and obstructions.

When I read the pamphlet, I was amazed to see that every single symptom I had been complaining of was listed with such specificity that I wondered if my parents printed this up just to make me feel better. Every type of food that made me ill was listed and popcorn was at the top of the list. I was unhappy to discover that I had a chronic, incurable illness but I took some pride in the fact that I did in fact have a physical problem and that I was not crazy!

I suppose my parents must have telephoned the psychologist to tell him that I was hospitalized and subsequently diagnosed with Crohn's Disease. As a result, a few days after the above revelation, he telephoned me in the hospital. He was very cordial at first and asked several questions regarding my well-being. If he was a pool hustler, he had just let me win the first rack. He was, as always, "grandfatherly" in his approach and immediately made me feel comfortable acknowledging the difficulties that lay ahead in dealing with an incurable, chronic illness. After he asked all the polite questions and showed his apparent deep concern, he then said something which I will never forget and which has prevented me from ever again seeking psychological counseling. More specifically, after he gained my trust and confidence on the telephone he tried to sink the 8-Ball and said: "Michael, do you see what you did to yourself now?"

Besides wanting to rip out my intravenous lines, get in a car, find him and throw him out a skyscraper window, I felt manipulated, betrayed and vulnerable. It was a complicated and intense feeling which I had never experienced up until that point in my life nor have I since. I felt violated by the question, its implications and his complete insensitivity to my struggles. My response was not even verbal. I simply yanked the phone out of the wall and began to cry thinking that I was alone in life and in the struggles that lie ahead with this mysterious illness. I knew the psychologist was wrong but I couldn't seem to disconnect the trust I had placed in him from his advice. I was also concerned that he would somehow have influence over my family and their opinion of me and my ability to battle this illness. Luckily, my parents and sisters immediately comforted me and my friends rallied around what they perceived as my toughness to withstand such a brutal ordeal.

That psychologist's bedside manner almost broke my family and me but I believed in myself and my observations about my body. I was also lucky in that the pamphlet validated my complaints. However, I could not have overcome the situation without my parent's support because of the blind trust I had placed in the psychologist. To that extent, parents need to be particularly aware of their child's complaints and the manner in which physicians address them. There are doctors who, for whatever reason, are too willing to blame all kinds of maladies on the mind. Sometimes they are right but when they are wrong your child can be scarred for life. Observe the interaction between your child and the doctor and make sure your child is comfortable with the manner he or she is being treated. More importantly, unless you have a reason to think otherwise, always trust your child's instincts about the doctor. Also, barring a problem with technical competency, stay away from the "best Park Avenue" specialist if your child is happy with the local specialist because good bedside manner can go a long way to healing a sick child.

My experience with that psychologist was positive for me in that I learned to trust myself and I discovered my solid foundation of family and friends. It has also made me acutely aware of the inevitable periods of self-doubt experienced by children afflicted with Crohn's Disease. Having learned the painful lesson that doctors can even trigger this self-doubt, I try to share my perspective with kids and their parents about these types of issues at CCFA symposiums and support group meetings. The downside to this experience is that I have never again sought psychological counseling despite having many friends who prosper immensely from such treatment.

As for the gastroenterologist, he had the strange habit of talking about my condition with my parents rather than with me. For example, I remember lying in bed looking outside my door and I saw him asking my mother various questions and her, apparently in response, pointing to various parts of her stomach. I didn't understand what was happening so when my mother came into my room I asked her if perhaps she had been experiencing abdominal problems. She said she wasn't but the doctor was asking her where it hurt me and she was trying to give him an idea of what my complaints had been up until that point. To me, that was akin to malpractice because I was 21 years old and fully entitled to complete access to my physician. More importantly, I was concerned that my mother's description could somehow be setting me up for some sort of surgery that perhaps I didn't need!

The next day when I saw the gastroenterologist, who incidentally happened to have the personality of a handball, I straightened him out and my hysterectomy was called off! It is one thing for physicians to explain to parents of patients what's going on but it is another when they totally disregard a patient's rights regardless of whether that patient is a child or elderly individual. Children and elderly patients might not appear to appreciate what's happening but there is tremendous mental comfort associated with being treated with respect. As such, I believe bedside manner is incredibly important even if there is some doubt as to whether the patient can understand or appreciate the efforts directed toward them.

GIVE DOCTORS THE BENEFIT OF THE DOUBT?

Doctor's have a reputation for being condescending and arrogant but don't be so quick to judge them because in the hospital setting they are often dealing with intense, emergent, life-threatening and emotional scenarios. Keep this in mind when your doctor is late attending to your concerns or seems rather distant when he or she examines you. Keep in mind that you could be one of those emergencies or life-threatening situations in the future. Have respect for these other patients because you will want their consideration when the situations are reversed. Notwithstanding the foregoing, some physicians, just like other people, are simply condescending and arrogant. These types, much like waiters at a trendy restaurant, walk away from you while you are in mid-sentence. This is an incredibly annoying habit and should be pointed out immediately because you are also a consumer who is entitled to the services for which you are paying. Additionally, in order to treat you, a physician must pay attention to your concerns. To do that, he or she must listen. If he or she is walking away while you are talking, they could therefore be compromising your care. Do not accept this behavior.

While not an example of physician behavior, the following example of arrogant, condescending behavior is typical of them. During my recent back surgery, I was standing in the hallway conversing with an occupational therapist when my surgeon's "Physician Assistant" stopped by to check on my progress. He was essentially the "point person" for my surgeon and as a result we had developed somewhat of a relationship. Before I could answer, he told me to be brief and "express myself in one sentence or less." I felt like I was a defendant in a case before television's "Judge Judy!" I was annoyed by his attitude but nevertheless complied because I didn't want to make a scene in front of the very attractive female occupational therapist with whom I was hoping to develop a relationship of a different kind. Perhaps he needed me to keep my comments brief because he couldn't possibly comprehend a more complicated description? I don't know the answer to that question but his comment belonged in a courtroom not a hospital. I have since had other dealings with him and he has been nothing but professional, competent and compassionate. If he reads this book, all I can say is that his comment, and not him, provided an excellent example for this chapter.

FOLLOW-UP/AFTERCARE

Physician follow-up is an extremely important aspect of your care. Surgeons may mechanically fix your problem but you are responsible for a large part of the healing and recovery. In some instances this involves a structured physical/occupational therapy program. In other instances, it is simply rest, diet and medication. In any case, be honest and follow-up. Perhaps the following story will illustrate my point.

After undergoing day-op orthopedic surgery on my left knee, my orthopedic surgeon told me to rest for several days and then contact him for a follow-up exam. Shortly thereafter, he planned to initiate physical therapy. Unfortunately, two days after my knee surgery, I had an intestinal obstruction due to an intense flare-up of my Crohn's Disease. As a result, I was hospitalized for several weeks at the end of which I underwent an abdominal resection operation. During this hospital stay the orthopedic surgeon's office occasionally left messages on my telephone answering machine pleading for me to come in for a follow-up visit. Eventually, I notified them about the abdominal surgery. Accordingly, we tentatively scheduled an appointment for several weeks after my discharge.

When I was ultimately discharged, I was instructed not to perform any strenuous activities for two (2) months. As part of my discharge instructions, I was counseled on the appropriate manner to resume sexual relations with my girlfriend. Given my large abdominal incision and Italian girlfriend, my physicians were concerned about such activity putting too much pressure on the wound thus rupturing the incision. They instructed me to only partake in those sexual positions in which my body was supported by my knees. Technically, they referred to this position as the "Kneeling Position." The upside to this position was that my abdominal incision remained in tact but the downside, as I was to find out, was that my entire bodyweight rested on my knees.

Several days after I was discharged I began to have relations with my girlfriend in the recommended position. However, the weight bearing began to cause an abrasion on my knee - particularly the knee where I had the arthroscopic surgery. This abrasion was apparently the result of my skin rubbing against the carpet. I didn't notice the abrasion at first but several weeks later my left knee was swollen and red. Coincidentally, my orthopedic surgeon was leaving messages every few days as he felt I was sufficiently recovered to finally follow-up with him. However, I was now too embarrassed to see him because I didn't know how to explain this swollen and infectious-looking condition. Eventually, the knee started looking so bad that I had no choice but to go back for the follow-up visit.

When he examined me, he was perplexed and called in his partners because he had never seen such a condition resulting from arthroscopic surgery. I was not forthcoming with how this condition occurred and told him that this is how my knee had looked since the surgery. He immediately became extremely concerned and ordering blood tests, x-rays, a bone scan and MRI. He also took Polaroid pictures of my knee because he thought this would be an interesting case to present to other doctors at medical conferences. Somehow I didn't think my girlfriend's father would appreciate the publicity.

My aversion to death by publicity, fear of needles and respect for my doctor's diligence made me confess. When we left the treating room and sat in his office I offered him the following deal: I would tell him the cause of the problem if he promised to destroy the Polaroid pictures. He was tentative but agreed. When I explained, he burst out in laughter. With a poker face, he then called in his partners and asked each for a diagnosis. They were hesitant but each began rattling off ridiculous medical jargon and tentative solutions only to be eventually interrupted with the real cause of the problem. It was very funny. Luckily, I was treated with simple antibiotics and the swelling and abrasions healed shortly thereafter. I suppose somewhere several times a year I am the butt of many jokes regarding what appeared to be a strange complication of simple arthroscopic surgery.

With respect to follow-up, that orthopedic surgeon was excellent because he actually followed-up with me. Maybe he was protecting himself but mostly I believe he cared about my well-being. Another unique experience I had with physician follow-up occurred during my recent back surgery and involved a unique follow-up interplay between myself and my physician. More specifically, I was home recuperating but grew concerned about the persistence of a particular pain located in the general area of the bone fusion. I called my surgeon but he was in surgery so I left a detailed message with his office manager. She assured me he would call me at some point during the day. Sure enough, about an hour later he called. However, I was in the shower. He got my voice mail and left me a detailed message specifically responsive to my concerns. The essence of his message was that my pain was normal and that unless the wound was red I needn't worry about it. He also indicated he would try me again later to speak with me directly.

His voice mail message answered my questions and completely alleviated my concerns. Nevertheless, about an hour later he called again and reached me personally. He repeated almost word for word his message but felt it important to personally speak with me because I was concerned. Whether he was operating that day or seeing patients in his office, calling me again was unnecessary. I did not expect it and was impressed by his interest, sincerity, compassion and follow-through. It was a simple follow-up phone call but I will never forget it. He is an excellent physician who, to the extent it involved his expertise, also demonstrated his comprehensive and compassionate follow-up during my turbulent physical rehabilitation detailed in Chapter 8.

PAY YOUR DOCTOR BILLS

I am not familiar with a physician's ethical obligations to treat indigent patients but if you are rendered a service you should pay for it. Physicians usually do not address this issue with patients because if they did I imagine some people might question their moral make-up and conflict of interest. However, there is nothing immoral about expecting to yield the fruits of one's labor. Nevertheless, physicians typically assign office personnel these collection duties so as to create separation between patient care and business dealings. However, physicians are human. To that extent, it would not be unreasonable for a physician to deny you care in the event you have no intention of paying him or her. I use the word "intention" because I have found that this seems to be all that most physicians require. They understand how expensive health care is and just ask that you make an attempt to pay. In some cases this may require sending $25 per month for several years while in others it might consist of making a sizeable flat fee payment in exchange for a substantially discounted surgical bill.

By emphasizing a physician's right to payment, I do not mean to imply that a physician will compromise care because of a deadbeat patient. Just keep in mind that physicians are human (except the ones who think there're God) and could be affected when the value of their services are ignored or taken for granted. I have been fairly critical of physicians and their practices. However, as a person with a chronic illness and substantial medical bills, my general experience with them regarding payment flexibility has been excellent. Treat their bills seriously, and they will work with you. A good example of this strategy is detailed in Chapter 9 regarding my "good faith" payment to the physician who performed the diagnostic tests for which my insurance company refused to pay.

Chapter 5

REACHING OUT

INTERACTING WITH FAMILY, FRIENDS AND BUSINESS ASSOCIATES

Anybody can handle success; it's how you respond to failure that ultimately determines how successful you'll be.

During my first few hospitalizations, self-pity governed my behavior. Interacting with healthy family members, friends and business colleagues fueled the natural inclination to ask, "Why Me?" I felt like an innocent man imprisoned and the self-pity impeded my ability to fight. My anger and resentment unfairly tested friendships, manipulated loved one's affections and made me a difficult and unappreciative patient. Up until that point I always thought that bad "things" in life happened for a reason. I believed that there was always a lesson to be learned. However, with each hospitalization it became increasingly difficult to find the "lesson." Then it dawned on me - sometimes the lesson is that there is no lesson. Bad "things" just happen and adversity can be a random occurrence that takes no consideration of good deeds, kind personality traits or quality of character.

With the help of a few perceptive nurses and several memorable hospital stays, I finally tapped into my acquired wisdom and realized that self-pity was the failure I had to face in order to become successful as a patient. Facing it, however, meant substantially modifying my behavior in dealings with what in the hospital setting I refer to as, "The Outside World." That is, family, friends and business colleagues. Once I stopped asking "Why Me?" and began to make the best of it, my health improved, I was hospitalized less frequently and my relationships deepened. Whether you are chronically hospitalized or just in for "minor" surgery (which incidentally is surgery that is performed on someone else), successfully interacting with The Outside World is crucial to your care, recuperation, relationships and feeling of well-being.

THE IMPORTANCE OF AVOIDING SELF-PITY

Your ability to avoid self-pity will be put to the test every time you interact with The Outside World. How well you cope with hospital adversities not only determines your state of mind but also makes an imprint on your family, friends and business colleagues. If you choose to interact with The Outside World, this imprint is important because it will inevitably affect your reputation when you are back on your feet and functioning as a healthy person. Some people, fearing a perception of weakness, choose not to deal with The Outside World. They limit their contact to a select few whose love and affection is unconditional. I believe such conduct is a mistake because if you deal successfully with your family, friends and business colleagues you will have mastered the psychology of being a patient. You will have mastered what most people cannot. Thus, avoiding self-pity and bravely dealing with The Outside World will provide a lifelong foundation of strength that is not easily duplicated in normal life experience. If it's true that "how you respond to failure ... ultimately determines how successful you'll be," overcoming the raw vulnerability of being a hospital patient will provide exponential future success.

THE VULNERABILITY OF
TOO MUCH INFORMATION

Before you start interacting with The Outside World, however, you should decide just how much information you wish to share. Information you might release to your family might not be appropriate for friends. Conversely, the same is true. Interactions with business colleagues could have more "bottom-line" effects in that overcoming adversity is admired but perceptions of weakness and feelings of sympathy could negatively affect your professional reputation. Keep this in mind when you tell business associates of your upcoming surgery or when they phone you in the hospital and ask how you are feeling. I suggest you be as generic as possible and provide the same information to each person because in the business world a good client/confidant today could be a competitor/enemy tomorrow.

Sometimes, however, the disclosure of information is out of your control. This happened to me when I worked at a large law firm and my secretary put a vivid description of my condition on the law firm's e-mail system of 250 users. At first, I was upset with the disclosure because no matter how I fudged it I was unable to bill for the time spent in the hospital! Seriously, in that instance the immediate reward seemed to far outweigh the perceived risk because the cards, gifts, flowers and phone calls I received substantially lifted my spirits. However, my chronic condition became well known throughout the firm and as a result my future professional prospects there were compromised. In fairness, though, I was subsequently treated with the utmost respect by management and my peers. I also wasn't ever particularly interested in becoming a partner there anyway. Nevertheless, hindsight tells me I should have instructed the secretary to be more discrete. That secretary and I stay in touch primarily because of the bond we developed during my various hospitalizations but had I been more interested in a future at the firm the price of that friendship could have been costly. Be careful.

THE BENEFITS OF FREQUENT HOSPITALIZATIONS

With respect to friends and family, the approach is much more complicated. Prior to being diagnosed with Crohn's Disease, I lived my life treating people in the manner I wished to be treated. When I became ill and largely dependent on the good deeds of others, I was fortunate in that family and friends were there to help me along. Upon my acceptance of anticipated chronic dependencies, I became more sensitive to being a better son, brother, friend and colleague because I felt as if I needed to store good deeds in reserve so that I would not feel guilty when my dependent situation required a substantial withdrawal. As a result, I became more attentive to the needs of my family and friends. When I finally became relatively healthy and free of consistent hospitalizations, I suddenly realized my friendships were deep, unconditional, multi-faceted and based on mutual respect. While I would have preferred a different path, I have thus benefited tremendously from dealing successfully with a chronic illness and frequent hospitalizations.

While my relationships are much richer because of my hospitalizations, I also have fewer relationships. This screening process is a result of disappointing reactions by friends and family to various hospitalizations. I am told this happens to you as you get older anyway, but it happened to me at an early age because of the extreme situations brought on by my illness. People say if you have no expectations, you won't be disappointed. This philosophy may be technically true but I believe it is a sad way to live life. Maybe you shouldn't have expectations of business colleagues, distant relatives or friendly acquaintances, but do have them of friends and loved ones. After all, isn't that secure feeling the ultimate privilege of calling someone a friend or loved one? Unless you are hospitalized for more than a few days you will not be in a position to experience this scenario. But, if you are hospitalized for any significant amount of time, people are bound to disappoint you. On the other hand, they can also surprise you. As I have found the surprise-to-disappointment ratio to be tenfold, just try to maintain an "even keel" and all will work out fine.

TELEPHONE ETIQUETTE

When you do not feel like speaking to people, take the telephone off the hook. When you do speak on the telephone, be careful what you say because the drugs you are taking may influence much of what you are saying or thinking. This could tend to make you emotional or euphoric. Therefore, keep the telephone conversations brief and upbeat. This is extremely important in the event you decide to make telephone calls for business purposes. By way of example, the rigors of my law practice require me to make business calls during hospital stays. I try to have my secretary make as many calls as possible, but sometimes it is unavoidable and I must make the call myself. If possible, I approach the call as if I am at a pay phone away from the office. However, that's sometimes risky due to the background hospital noises. In the event I sense the "pay phone" approach could come off disingenuous, I simply tell the client I am hospitalized but try to put off dealing with the specifics. Sometimes, however, that is not possible because my client's rights might be comprised by my continued confinement. In such an event, I inform the client of the possible consequences and recommend another attorney. Salespeople might have a harder time doing this but clients will appreciate the candor and may even reward you with loyalty and long term business.

<u>VISITORS</u>

Being visited in the hospital is a unique experience because it not only exposes your vulnerability but also reflects the bond between you and the visitor. Visitors will see you in compromising positions both literally and figuratively. These visits then become somewhat intimate. Therefore, you might want to screen out who is permitted to get such a view. This is also applicable to visits by children. I am not married and do not have children but I have four (4) nephews. From time-to-time, each has visited me in the hospital. I always enjoy their visits but cringe after they leave because I do not like for them to see me so physically compromised. For me, it depends upon the ailment and how far along I am in the recuperative process. For example, during my most recent back surgery hospitalization I was in too much pain to see anybody but my parents. Candidly, I did not want to scream and cry in the presence of my macho friends or emotional siblings. However, one of my closest friends stopped by each of the first few days on his way home from work. I am told my appearance and condition visibly shook him. We are very close and possibly closer because of this experience but it was too much for him to handle for I don't think he will ever forget the pain and suffering I experienced. I would never want to make such a lasting impression upon my nephews.

Surprise visits should be particularly discouraged because of this vulnerability. For example, in the event your surgery affects your bowel habits you may not want visitors to pop in unannounced because they may catch you at an inappropriate time. However, just like anything else that is not an exact science, sometimes the opposite is true and a surprise visit could be just what the doctor ordered. I was the beneficiary of such a visit during my recent back surgery. More specifically, it was lunchtime and the prospect of eating the eclectic hospital mix of matzo ball soup, pizza and Spanish rice made me want to puke. Just as I was about to begin eating this "prison" food, I received a phone call from one of my uncles. While I have always enjoyed his company, geographical logistics have put constraints on our relationship. However, each time I am in the hospital he seems to say or do something that no one else does and for that reason we have a special bond. This time he told me he was downstairs in the lobby and wanted to join me for lunch. Since he works in the hospital administration industry and is familiar with the quality, or lack thereof, of the hospital food, he then offered to bring up whatever I wanted to eat. I told him I was fantasizing of a corned beef sandwich, knish, potato salad and a creme soda. Within thirty minutes he was up in my room unwrapping my fantasy. We ate, laughed and talked. It was like an old friend stopping by at work and made me feel as if I was not confined but merely in a transitional stage to a new office.

Contrary to my encouragement of general expectations, be careful not to expect much during a hospital visit. Loved ones tend to make predictable visits but your friends will amaze you. I have always found this to be the most interesting part of the hospital stay because it is almost like a theatrical play that writes itself. The people who care most seem to fight for the leading parts. Generally, though, people don't know what to do other than to show up and pay their respects. I find it most comfortable to reassure my visitors that while I appreciate their visits I do not want the conversation to focus on my ailments and me. I certainly discuss my ailments but I try to maintain and continue whatever relationship I had with that person prior to my hospitalization. I emphasize this point to my family and friends because my constant hospitalizations sometimes make me feel ostracized from society. To that extent, I seek normalcy when I am visited so that, but for the location, my interactions are normal.

I sincerely appreciate the lengths to which visitors have gone to accomplish this request. Particular kudos to some of the women I have dated! Two of my closest buddies have mastered this normalcy request by continuing their digs on my golf game, dating life and NFL football picks. One has even admitted that he came to visit me only because he was trying to get the phone number of, as he referred to her, a "hot" floor nurse. This guy has obviously seen too many "Seinfeld" episodes! Notwithstanding the foregoing, there are times when you simply need to cry and complain about your predicament. That's perfectly normal. Just be careful to whom you expose this vulnerability and don't ever ask, "Why Me?" because there is somebody or something, somewhere, answering, "Why Not?"

Chapter 6

DEALING WITH THE INSIDE WORLD

ROOMMATES, PRIVACY AND CREATING A COMFORTABLE ENVIRONMENT

The preceding chapters provide general suggestions for coping and dealing with the practical and emotional aspects of a hospital stay. However, certain aspects of a hospital stay warrant more particular attention because they more vividly demonstrate the vulnerability and unique hospital environment. This chapter highlights a few of these personal aspects and offers some suggestions for minimizing their de-humanizing emotional effects.

PRIVACY

The most uncomfortable aspects of the hospital stay usually revolve around privacy issues. These privacy issues typically involve bathroom scenarios, bathing and overall establishment and protection of one's "space." These issues in turn often stem from the hospital's design whereby patients are roomed with other patients. Dealing with your pain, loneliness, depression and other associated aspects of the hospital stay are difficult enough. Throw in the idiosyncrasies of a roommate with the sudden complete loss of privacy and an intolerable situation could result. In order to prevent such a scenario, you need to employ techniques that preserve your individuality and/or establish a comfortable environment.

TOILETS

As most of my hospitalizations have been the result of abdominal ailments, using the bathroom has been a vital part of my hospital experience. Since we all use the bathroom in the same way, a technique to individualize the experience doesn't help. However, I need to feel comfortable in the bathroom and not as if I am defecating at a rest stop on the New Jersey Turnpike. To that end, I ensure my "comfortability" in this area by asking my nurse for as many "Isopropyl Alcohol" "packets" as possible. These little two (2") inch square "packets" are designed to be used to sterilize injection sites but I use them to sterilize the toilet seat. Granted, they are difficult to use in a pinch but if you have enough time they work well.

BATHING

Unless you are permitted to shower, bathing can be a very dehumanizing experience. Due to hospital constraints that prevent you from showering in lavish surroundings or bathing in a jacuzzi, "comfortability" techniques won't help in this area. Therefore, I suggest you employ an individualized technique that humanizes the experience and makes you feel more like the person you were before you entered the hospital. Individualization techniques aside, the choice is, "To Be Bathed?" or "Not To Be Bathed?" In order to maintain your cleanliness, appearance and self-respect, you must bathe. However, you can either be bathed or wash yourself. Selfbathing in the hospital is a very slow, mechanical and de-humanizing process but in my opinion it beats the alternative of having a complete stranger do to you what he or she least likely prefers to do. Besides, the last thing I want a disgruntled employee to do is scrub my genitalia!

At the risk of sounding like a Sesame Street instructor communicating via song, "This Is How I Wash Myself," "Wash Myself," "Wash Myself," "Wash Myself ...," typically a nurse or nurses' assistants fills a basin with warm water and brings it to my bed. I make sure she also brings a washcloth, plenty of towels and a bar of soap. I try to pick a time of the day when I do not anticipate any interruptions. While I have outlined the hospital schedule in a previous chapter, anticipating peace in the hospital is still a crapshoot. In any event, I pull the curtain completely around my bed for privacy and lay a few towels down on the floor. I then put the washcloth around the soap, dip it into the basin and begin to wash my body in specific parts basically applying the same techniques used in washing a car. Then I put the washcloth back in the basin (without the soap), ring it out, re-wet it, and then use it to rinse off the soap on the particular area I just scrubbed. Throughout the process I am careful to avoid getting any water on my incision and take into account any physical limitations caused by my surgery or condition.

Whether you bathe yourself or are bathed by a nurse, it is demeaning. However, if you individualize the task you will have taken the first steps toward "humanization" and away from being referred to as "the patient in 12B."

<u>ROOMMATES</u>

Relationships with roommates are always interesting. Generally, there are two extremes: the patients who prefer to keep to themselves; and the "Felix Unger" types. For the most part, the roommate relationship is an insignificant element to your recovery. Nonetheless, some relationships have lasting effects. For example, when I was first diagnosed with Crohn's Disease, I had a roommate with the same condition who was about ten years older than I was. We didn't talk much but I overheard his interactions with physicians, nurses and his family. He was very sick with no end to his suffering in sight. He was also an attorney and practiced on his own because the unpredictability and frequency of his hospitalizations forced him to leave a large firm. His health problems were disrupting his life in every imaginable fashion. Yet, he discarded using medications that would ease his pain so that he could stay alert for his business, wife and children. I, on the other hand, was in denial about my Crohn's Disease and did all I could to numb the physical and emotional pain. Having overheard my conversations with the hospital staff, he sensed my immaturity and one day came to talk to me. He constructively pointed out my denial and suggested something to the extent that I instead "be a man – not a kid" and deal with the illness head-on. I don't remember his name and can't recall his face, but I will never forget the manner in which he conducted himself. His courage, convictions, perspective and attitude had a great effect upon me. I'd like to think I now conduct myself in a similar fashion.

As evidenced above, you can learn a great deal from roommates. Granted, it took me a while to comprehend the above lesson and accordingly modify my behavior but sometimes there could be more immediate effects. For instance, a younger patient might remind an older patient of the body's capacity for resiliency. Conversely, the wisdom and perspective of an older patient with respect to illness, confinement and hospital frustrations can be invaluable to a young adult dealing with serious illness for the first time. Therefore, don't be distant and don't be like "Felix Unger," just listen and, if appropriate, talk to your roommate – you might learn something.

Interacting with roommates can also trigger great emotions because you could be forced to think about issues far more significant than your own. This has happened to me on numerous occasions primarily because I have often been placed on the floor with the open bed as opposed to the one most suitable to my condition. As a result, I have been paired with patients suffering from a myriad of conditions with consequences ranging from life threatening to minor inconveniences. Often, I sat up at night and talked to them about their condition, whether it was a broken leg, appendicitis, heart ailments, blood disease or cancer. Usually the ones with the more serious conditions stand out in my memory – except for one.

<u>DEALING WITH DEATH</u>

More specifically, my recollection is that this middle-aged patient had an intense bout with asthma but was nowhere near a life-threatening situation. I had just moved to Boston and had no friends in the area. To that extent, we got along well because I suppose I was lonely and more open to talking than I had been in the past with other roommates. One night while we were laughing and commiserating about our respective situations as if we were simply waiting to be fixed and set free back into life, he suddenly had a heart attack. Immediately, monitors and beepers sounded and doctors and nurses rushed into the room. He died several minutes later - five (5') feet from my bed. I never saw him again because the resuscitation efforts prevented me from peeking in and he was thereafter immediately transferred to another area of the hospital. I knew him as well as I knew any one else in the State of Massachusetts. I was twenty-six (26) years old and frightened. I don't know any helpful suggestions for easing the emotions brought on by death. I can tell you, however, that as a hospital patient you must be aware that it can occur to anyone, at anytime. Perhaps simply that awareness will help.

In another instance, I got to know a roommate who had a rare blood disease. He was in his early forties and but for the monitors and tubes attached to his body appeared healthy. Not only did I get to know him but I got to know his family because his wife and children came in with holiday food as we were both hospitalized during the Thanksgiving holiday. In the middle of the Thanksgiving Day football games, he was visited by his doctor and told that there was no cure for his illness. He and his wife were then delicately told that he would die within a few months. I didn't want to let on that I heard the prognosis and in our ensuing conversations he never told me. He kept a stiff upper lip and kept telling me that I should not be depressed about being hospitalized during the holiday. A few days later I was transferred to the medical floor so that my Crohn's Disease could be treated more conveniently. I didn't know what to say to him when I left. I knew he was going to die, he knew he was going to die, but he didn't know that I knew. I casually said, "Take care," but meant a whole lot more.

On a lighter note, hospital roommates can make you laugh. One of my funniest roommate experiences occurred when I overheard the interplay between my roommate, an incredibly obese diabetic, and a resident debating the merits of yet another rectal examination. The patient protested the bodily invasion but the resident insisted it was necessary. The patient eventually gave in and rolled over for the exam. However, his obesity made it difficult for the resident to locate the point of entry. Finally after several failed attempts at insertion, the resident said to him, "Can you fart and at least give me a clue!" I had to put a pillow over my face for three hours to control my laughter.

ORDERLIES

In keeping with the lighter close of this chapter, take the time to get to know the orderlies and transporting staff. They have difficult jobs and will appreciate the effort. I have found them also eager to help create a more personal or palatable environment. Much like the cinematic images of Mafia "Dons" in prison eating caviar and drinking champagne, I enjoy the challenge of creating a comfortable environment in the hospital setting. While my family and friends attempt to satisfy my every whim, sometimes I feel uncomfortable being specific with them about my desires. Besides, I can't exactly ask my parents or sisters to round me up a hospital poker game!

Whether I have sought the current "Sports Illustrated" issue or a corned beef sandwich from a local delicatessen, orderlies and transporting staff members always come through in a big way. Granted, I compensate them for "running" these "errands" but their efforts are probably against hospital rules and they are nevertheless extremely reliable and understanding of my plight. They also take the load off my friends and family and make me feel less dependent. That's valuable to me so I try to treat them generously. You would be wise to do the same.

Chapter 7

THE EMERGENCY ROOM

No hand-holding, no cuddling, no candles and no promises. Beer instead of wine and "McDonalds" instead of a well-cooked steak dinner. The emergency room is the fast food, no-nonsense department of the hospital. The staff's philosophy is akin to "Lov'em and Leav'em." It is an area of the hospital which brings out the best and worst in medical care. However, in this era of managed care where physicians won't admit a patient unless a butcher knife is ten (10) inches embedded into the chest cavity, more people than ever before are familiar with the hospital setting through their interaction with the emergency room. The emergency room has emerged from the "front lines" of medical care to becoming both a source of primary care and a substitute for patients who ordinarily should be hospitalized. The consequential over-crowding, pressure, eclectic patient population and increased expectations make for a unique environment that requires distinct coping skills.

TIPS ON GETTING TREATED

The definition of success as a patient in the emergency room is merely "To Be Treated." To that end, I suggest the following:

1. Be persistent;
2. Whenever possible, vomit <u>on</u> hospital personnel;
3. Irregardless of your degree of pain, scream as if you just found out your mother-in-law is moving in; and

4. Faint or hyperventilate.

There is no emergency room busy season or slow time since people have accidents and do stupid things all the time. Whether it's an unfortunate victim of a car crash or a cute, but incredibly stupid, little boy with a piece of a crayon stuck up his nose (I was cute though), the emergency room is always busy. To that extent, you will need to follow the above instructions in order to obtain prioritized care. While I doubt this is printed in medical school textbooks, the general rule in the emergency room is that the loudest person gets treated first. Exceptions are made for those patients who faint, hyperventilate or vomit. However, the vomit must actually strike a member of the emergency room staff to be prioritized ahead of the "fainters" and "hyperventalators." Exceptions are also made for patients who persistently scream of pain. However, "Oh My God, It's Killing Me" won't rise to the exception level. You will need to be more creative such as, "I'm In So Much Pain, I Could Sit Through Two (2) Hours Of PBS Television Programming!" or "If You Don't Give Me Something For The Pain Soon, I Will Leave, Quit My Job At The Post Office And Come Back!"

Seriously, I have tremendous respect for emergency room personnel because of what they are required to do and the conditions in which they are required to function. I also admire their willingness to accept the awesome responsibility of being in the "front lines." However, my "prioritized care" suggestions are not far-fetched and are actually based on personal experience. Take the feeling of "pain" as an example. It is a typical complaint of emergency room patients but is usually intermittent and does not occur every second. Sometimes a movement or activity triggers it, other times it is spasmodic. However, once you acknowledge to emergency room personnel that the pain "comes and goes," your priority will have "came and went." It's funny but it's logical as emergency room personnel must be initially concerned with only the life-threatening or most serious cases. Therefore, if you have pain, scream! I am not encouraging you to lie or exaggerate your condition. I am just suggesting that you clearly emphasize the severity of your condition. However, if another patient seems more deserving of immediate care, be considerate and tell the attendant.

My first truly life-threatening but non-ambulance visit to an emergency room was due to an intestinal "obstruction." While shut down for business, the natural peristalsis of my intestine nonetheless forced air and fluid to continue through and attempt to penetrate the occluded or "obstructed" portion of my intestine. When I began to experience the resulting child labor-like pain, I was at my parent's house. They called my gastroenterologist and were told to immediately take me to the hospital in Manhattan at which he had admitting privileges. According to my doctor, my condition warranted immediate attention because the obstruction could cause an intestinal perforation. If that happened, he emphasized that I could die. When we arrived at the emergency room, it was filled-to-capacity with a broad range of patients. There were people bleeding from stab wounds, children crying and weekend warriors with knee and back problems. Given my perilous condition, my doctor had called ahead to notify the emergency room of my arrival. Despite my hair-raising screams and his instructions to admit me, I was told to sit in the waiting room.

My father, not being able to tolerate my suffering, literally carried me to the front desk and begged for the attendant to reconsider and facilitate my treatment and admission. She hardly flinched, however, and with the calmness of a librarian asked me for my insurance card. When I started to reach for my wallet, the pain made me double-over and I continued screaming. My father reached for my wallet and tried to find my insurance card. At the same time he pleaded for the attendant to summon a doctor immediately. The attendant said that there was an approximate one (1) hour wait. As my pain was spasmodic, I had several lucid pain-free intervals. During one, I sarcastically remarked, "Boy, the food must be really good!" She gave me a puzzled look. I then yelled, "I'm not here for dinner reservations, I am having an intestinal obstruction!" Before she countered with a snide remark, the pain kicked in again. However, this time it reached an unprecedented level.

WHEN ALL ELSE FAILS, VOMIT!

Along with the unprecedented pain came that strange anticipatory feeling in my gut. I sensed that something was about to projectile out of my body; I just couldn't pinpoint the exact second. (In case you've never vomited, that strange anticipatory feeling is similar to the one immediately prior to male orgasm – except completely different!!!) As I was attempting to bear down on the pain and maintain my composure, the attendant began asking me mundane medical background questions. I felt like my body was about to explode. Much to the chagrin of the attendant, I was right. I vomited all over her desk but, luckily, some rebounded and landed on her blouse. Then I passed out. When I awoke several hours later, I was in a bed admitted to the medical floor. I'm not sure whether it was my screaming, vomiting or fainting but I have a feeling either one on its own would have gotten me that room. However, I'm not sure the vomiting would have worked without the fortuitous rebound. Ergo, my advice to aim!

LISTEN TO YOUR BODY

While vomiting, fainting and creative screaming will usually get you treated, persistency is medically important. Although emergency room personnel routinely save lives, sometimes their care is designed to temporarily resolve symptoms rather than alleviate problems. They are certainly capable of solving problems. It's just that often they can't because of too many patients and too little time. As a result, you must be persistent in your pursuit of a resolution to a problem even if you must go to the emergency room several times for the same problem. This persistency is even more important with the advent of managed care because many patients seeking primary care now look to the emergency room. However, don't forget that being discharged from the emergency room does not necessarily mean that your problem has been solved. Some patients mistakenly make this assumption because emergency room personnel are extremely competent, comforting and thorough. Others make the assumption because they are lazy or cost-conscious and don't want to follow-up with their primary care physician.

By way of example, I was recently "rushed" to the hospital by my secretary for severe back pain. I suspected that I had a kidney stone because I was unable to urinate and was experiencing intense pain in a specific area of my lower back. I begged my secretary to drive 100 miles an hour and "rush" me to the hospital but probably because I was paying her by the hour she wouldn't drive faster than the speed limit. When we arrived in the emergency room, the staff quickly attended to me since I had classic kidney stone symptoms. Due to my inability to urinate, they immediately catheterized me and the pain was substantially reduced. However, all diagnostic tests for kidney stones were negative. The assumption was that I had probably passed an almost microscopic stone while I was catheterized. I was fine with that conclusion since the pain was gone.

After a few hours, a nurse took out the catheter and told me that I would be discharged after I "voided." As soon as the urge to urinate came upon me, I went to the bathroom. Just as I was about to enter the bathroom, the nurse whispered to me that I might experience a little "discomfort" due to irritation from the Foley Catheter. When nurses, as opposed to physicians, use the word "discomfort" it is usually just that - an accurate description of minor irritation or pain. Having had several Foley Catheters in the past, I was familiar with this slight "after-effect" discomfort. Much to my surprise, however, when I began to urinate it felt as if razor blades were coming out of my penis! Hearing my screams, the nurse came into the bathroom and assumed that either I was acting out a scene from the movie "Something About Mary," or I was simply extremely sensitive to pain. I complained of the "razor blade" abnormality, but she just thought I was a wimp who couldn't handle the minor "discomfort" after-effect. She was obviously studying to be a physician as she had a firm grasp of their arrogant "discomfort" description. As a result, I was discharged but told to follow-up with a urologist. Despite my razor blade description, my urologist couldn't fit me in to his schedule for a few days. I suppose his schedule was booked up with more serious patients like those urinating jagged-edged javelons!

I went to sleep when I can home but was awakened in the middle of the night with the urge to "void." When I went to the bathroom I began to urinate and that good old nostalgic "razor blade" feeling came upon me once again. Obviously there was something seriously wrong but I initially felt uncomfortable going back to the emergency room since the staff concluded that I was fine. Nevertheless, I telephoned an ambulance and was back at the hospital within fifteen minutes. Luckily, tests revealed that I had a kidney stone lodged in my urethra thus explaining the "razor blade" sensation. The stone was apparently undetectable during my first emergency room visit because it was midway between my kidney and urethra.

I imagine there were more sophisticated tests that could have nevertheless correctly diagnosed my condition during the first visit. However, the combination of the difficult diagnosis, time constraints, high number of patients and limited supply of personnel made it unreasonable to expect such testing to be performed in the emergency room. Besides, during the first visit my primary complaints were only severe pain in my lower back and an inability to urinate. These complaints were addressed and completely resolved. The resulting "razor blade" sensation could have been, as they suspected, simply an overreaction to the removal of the catheter. However, my persistency was the difference. Thanks to my urologist not comprehending the sensation of a razor blade emanating from my penis, this story is also a good example of the increasing use of the emergency room for both urgent and primary care. In short, don't be afraid to go back to the emergency room for the same problem even if doing so is embarrassing.

<u>CALL YOUR PHYSICIAN BEFORE ARRIVING</u>

It is also a good idea to phone both your physician and the emergency room before you arrive so that both are aware of your intended arrival. Such notification can expedite your care. However, depending upon the time of day or night, this can also annoy physicians. Do not be concerned, however, because if they did not want to be bothered in the middle of the night they would have chosen another occupation. Nevertheless, be prepared for an attitude when you arrive at the hospital particularly if it is 3:00 AM and your ailment seems to have a history of inconvenient timing. Obstetricians are comfortable with this type of inconvenient timing because women give birth on nature's timetable. Strangely, other doctors do not share this logical perspective about appendicitis, kidney stones, intestinal obstructions, asthma attacks, etc. Are you not supposed to have a heart attack in the middle of the night? Is your ulcer not allowed to bleed whenever it wants? This is a touchy issue with me because I have had horrible experiences with physicians in the middle of the night as my Crohn's Disease has a mind of its own and often flares up with a total disregard for appropriate timing.

While I might appear critical of specialty physicians with respect to emergency room visits, most of the difficulties can be avoided if patients are considerate. Do not page your doctor at 3:00 AM if you think you are bloated and feeling constipated. Do not page your doctor at 3:00 AM if you need cough medicine. However, do page your doctor at 3:00 AM if you have shortness of breath, severe abdominal pain or shooting pains down your arm. Be smart. Take advantage of your physician's 24-hour accessibility but do not abuse the privilege.

My cynicism aside, I have had some pleasant experiences after being met in the emergency room at the most inconvenient times by the friendly face of my specialty physician. While he or she did not enjoy waking up in the middle of the night, they understood my illness and their job with respect thereto. Their compassion under the adverse circumstances was remarkable. However, I had one experience with a physician meeting me in the emergency room that to this day still concerns me about being a patient in need of emergency care. In keeping with the design of this book, this story could have been included in the "Physician" chapter but it belongs here because it occurred in an emergency room - a place I have come to count on for vital health care - 24 hours a day, 365 days a year.

AN ABBERATION: MY ONE TRULY HORRIBLE EXPERIENCE

This story is not an accurate reflection upon my experiences in the emergency room because, other than long waiting periods and the vomit episode, it is the only negative experience I can remember. This is significant because I have been brought to emergency rooms on at least thirty-five occasions, for a variety of conditions, in several different parts of the country, and at many different times of the day and night. Some visits were life threatening, others were merely run-of-the-mill ailments. In every instance, however, no matter where I went, the quality and consistency of care was excellent. Matter of fact, it is for this reason that people like myself with chronic illnesses that require unpredictable hospitalizations have been able to conduct normal social and professional lives (e.g. traveling). We do not live in fear of being hospitalized specifically because of the quality and dependability of emergency rooms and emergency room personnel. Therefore, try to look at the following story as the rare exception exposed for the benefit of spotlighting the high quality, consistent, compassionate and courteous care provided in emergency rooms around the country.

It was 1993 and I had been having a very difficult time with my Crohn's Disease. I had been obstructing almost on a daily basis. As a result, I was rushed by ambulance to the local New Jersey hospital on two different occasions within the same week at 2:00 AM and 4:00 AM, respectively. Unfortunately, each time the same gastroenterologist was "on call." He was not the physician I routinely saw in that "group" but he was the covering physician on these two occasions. Usually such established specialty groups had residents or fellows handling overnight "call." But this group, for some reason, was simply comprised of a few partners who shared overnight call in some pre-planned rotational schedule.

The first night he treated me competently. The second night, he was irritated. His irritation bothered me because it implied that I had some control over the circumstances. In fact, my lack of control was psychologically devastating to me. This in turn exacerbated my condition. While administering various medications during the second visit, he began to question the legitimacy of my complaints as if I actually enjoyed getting up at 4:00 AM for my second ride to the hospital in an ambulance within a week. I felt his accusations did not deserve to be legitimized by a denial so I just said nothing. In the "uncomfortablity" of silence, I noticed I showed up both nights in torn sweat pants and old t-shirts while he was impeccably dressed in Gucci shoes, designer slacks, expensive shirts and natty ties. I was his cash cow - a chronically ill patient with

95

disposable income. My mind began to race as his inhumane treatment of me apparently struck a nerve. I was acutely aware that patients like me made his life as financially comfortable as it was.

As the administration of medication was unsuccessful in relieving my pain, he grew extremely frustrated and began directly attacking my manhood by virtue of my inability to deal with the pain. At first, I was unable to verbally defend myself because narcotics and the continuing onset of intense spasmodic pain compromised my thought process and made me completely emotional. However, he persisted and did so in front of my parents, several nurses and other emergency room personnel. His words were biting and his tone was nasty. As if my pain, frustration and nightly ordeals weren't enough, a physician who suspected I enjoyed the attention, drugs or overall sensation of being a patient was treating me. While I imagine there are patients who fall into those categories, I clearly was not. Finally, the pain, utter frustration, emotional sensitivity and complete embarrassment made me cry. He then increased the intensity of his tirade and scolded me as if my crying somehow indicated my admission of guilt as to his allegations.

I eventually summoned up the strength to stand up and look him eye-to-eye hoping that eye contact would somehow convey my genuine pain and horror. Nevertheless, he continued to berate me like I was a little boy caught playing with matches. I pleaded with him to stop yelling at me but he was so intensely agitated that the veins were popping out of his neck. Out of total frustration, I attempted to punch him in the face. The nurses interceded and somehow he got away unscathed. I subsequently left the emergency room and made plans to see my gastroenterology group in New York a few days later. For fear of encountering him again in the New Jersey emergency room, I stopped eating until my New York appointment. My New York doctor immediately conducted several diagnostic tests and discovered I had <u>eight</u> intestinal obstructions. He was surprised I was still alive and walking not to mention functioning as an attorney! Within a few hours of the results, I scheduled surgery to repair the obstructions. Thanks to an excellent surgeon, I got my life back.

Some people take solace in being able to say "I Told You So," but I never got that opportunity because that gastroenterologist who mistreated me in the emergency room was part of a group practice represented by the law firm at which I was an associate. Not only was he dangerously wrong in his diagnosis but his actions made me fearful of being treated in emergency rooms. Nevertheless, as a peon at the law firm, I was dissuaded from filing a formal complaint with the appropriate authorities. That didn't stop me from thinking about him though. In fact, I thought about him when I contemplated writing this book. I also thought about him whenever I was too tired to finish paragraphs, pages and chapters. However, the resulting anger got me through and fueled my desire to finish this book and share my experiences with other patients. Looking back, with the publication of this book I guess I finally reported him to the proper authorities after all.

Chapter 8

BOUNCIN' BACK

PHYSICAL REHABILITATION, HANDLING SETBACKS AND GETTING OFF NARCOTICS

Last week I took her name off my mailbox
Threw out some shoes and clothes she left behind
I even took her picture off of my dresser
I believe these are very good signs. . .
I've got the urge to sing again
I've got the urge to dance
I can see myself again
Giving love just one more chance. . .
I'm finally bouncin' back

- Dennis Walker

These words are from the song, "Bouncin' Back," recorded by blues guitarist/vocalist Robert Cray denoting the often difficult but gradual empowering emergence from heartbreak. Its message of renewed self-awareness and inspiring resiliency, however, accurately describes the hospital patient recuperation process. This is the song that I think of the instant I leave the hospital and my non-slippered feet hit the pavement.

WHEN YOUR MIND MAKES PROMISES YOUR BODY CAN'T KEEP

Recuperating from illness, surgery and/or a hospital stay is difficult especially as you get older because your mind tends to make promises your body can't keep. Your mind wants to pick-up your granddaughter but your new plaque-free arteries and cardiologist prohibit you from doing so. Your mind wants to convert that boring twenty-minute treadmill walk into a run but your new knee and orthopedic surgeon tell you otherwise. As a result, patients are not the best judges of their recuperative powers. Even more importantly, the ups and downs of the recuperative process can be so emotionally tumultuous that excellent medical/surgical results can appear to be, at least temporarily, completely negated. For this reason, I put off writing this chapter until I was fully recuperated from my back surgery. This way, I could more objectively reflect upon the volatile nature of the recuperation process. Accordingly, in an attempt to finish this book, I was forced to travel to Club Med in Cancun, Mexico because I was told that would expedite my recuperation!

THE FIRST STEP TO RECUPERATION IS PSYCHOLOGICAL

While laying on the beach in Cancun, I read Jimmy Buffet's novel "A Pirate Looks At Fifty" and realized why it is important to recuperate and move on. Sure, it depressed me that I had screws holding my back together and scars on my stomach but as Mr. Buffet sees it each of these in the long run are only "Permanent Reminders of Temporary Feelings." That's why you must get on with your life. You can't wallow in your past misfortune because there are interesting people to meet, laughs to be had, relationships to be cherished, places to visit, books to read, music to listen to, business deals to close and adversities to conquer. Once I realized this, I began to relax, reflect and put some distance between my traumatic back surgery and the next chapter of my life. It was then, soon after I met my "therapeutic" new friends from Vancouver, Canada, when I knew I was ready to take the first steps toward recuperation. It was then when I also knew that the physical part of the rehabilitation could wait until I got home.

THE NEXT STEP
MIGHT TAKE A WHILE

While the preceding paragraph illustrates the psychological component of recuperation, the day-to-day aspects are dominated by physical and emotional challenges. Perhaps you can benefit from my recent experience regarding both. I came back from Cancun in mid-May of 1999 and fully anticipated finishing this book. However, I wanted to first enjoy the "privilege" to exercise again. It's a "privilege" because it can be taken away in an instant by a twist, pull, stretch or strain. For example, immediately prior to my trip to Cancun, my surgeon had given me medical clearance to exercise because my x-rays were perfect and I was completely pain-free. He said during my consultation that I could play golf, tennis and even jog lightly. I was so far ahead of schedule, especially considering how much pain I was in prior to surgery, that he practically considered me the "poster boy" for spine fusion surgery. What he didn't know before he so anointed me is that I am also the national spokesperson for the organization, "Give Me An Inch And I'll Take A Yard!"

The problem began immediately after I left his office and decided to take his advice. Keep in mind, I hadn't performed any exercise besides rehabilitative walking in approximately nine months. Therefore, I was careful to follow his advice except I attempted to play golf, tennis and jog lightly <u>all in the same afternoon</u>! Within a few hours after these exercises I was driven to the emergency room because of intense pain. My surgeon was not pleased but the emergency staff got a kick out of my sheer stupidity. Apparently my muscles rebelled against the sudden demand for performance. Within a few days my surgeon advocated that I begin physical therapy and learn how to begin to exercise safely. While my surgeon's physical therapy referral slip didn't specify my condition, in some sort of coded insurance language I'm sure it said: "This patient is a schmuck and I do not trust him making decisions about his recuperation."

Thanks to an excellent physical therapist and the assistance of a thorough and compassionate physiatrist, my muscular pain was quieted down and I was able to go to Cancun pain-free. However, I was warned not to partake in any exercises other than walking. When I came back from Cancun, my physical therapist began to increase the intensity of my therapy. We concentrated primarily on "range of motion" and "stabilization" exercises and I responded quite well. I began to once again get excited especially when I was able to increase my aerobic activities from walking on a treadmill to actually breaking a sweat on an elliptical training machine. It was now June and my recuperation seemed unstoppable as I inched closer toward my goals of running and exercising at the levels I was accustomed to prior to January's back surgery. I felt physically stronger and mentally sharper as I had endured, overcome and learned from a major rehabilitation setback prior to my trip to Cancun.

I imagine my physical therapist picked up on my confidence and as a result she increased my activity to standing/walking "thrusts" and "squats." This seemed rather much but by the looks of things I appeared to be ready. In fact, prior to progressing to these exercises, I had actually begun playing golf with my friends even walking all eighteen holes and had experienced no pain whatsoever. However, within fifteen minutes of performing these exercises, I was once again in excruciating muscular pain. What frightened me though was that this time the pain mimicked my pre-surgical complaints. I was devastated as I thought I somehow undid what my doctor had done.

As in the first setback, I had to again resume taking pain medications and muscle relaxers. The only comforting part about this set-back was that I knew exactly what type of exercise triggered it and that in the future I would refrain from such activities. However, the pain wasn't going away as quickly as it had during the previous setback and I was more than concerned. Luckily, however, after approximately two weeks of ultrasound treatments, massage therapy and intense heat compounds, the pain went away and I resumed exercising. I kept my surgeon abreast of the setback but he seemed unconcerned especially considering my high-strung personality and active life-style. He felt the surgery was successful but that I had irritable muscles that would heal only when they were good and ready.

While the squats and thrusts were off-limits, my physical therapist was intent on strengthening the muscles in my rear end. I was a little hesitant but the prospect of resuming to run, which can't be done without strengthening these muscles, convinced me to give it a go. These new exercises were less intense and less "resistance" oriented, but within 15 minutes of doing them I once again was in extreme pain. And so began my third setback. This time, however, the pain was completely intolerable. More importantly, I was emotionally spent from having endured the uncertainty of the prior setbacks. One week I was kicking my friends' butts on the golf course and the next I was laying on a heating pad all weekend watching television. As I was once again confined to my couch on a beautiful July weekend, I feared that a pattern was beginning to form and that I would never be able to exercise normally without experiencing extreme pain. I was also concerned that I was once again becoming dependent on dangerous and addictive medications.

<u>DON'T LOSE YOUR HEAD</u>

At this point, in July and August, I was calling my surgeon almost on a daily basis and probably driving him nuts. I went to see him and he insisted that I just continue on the medications and reiterated that this pain would eventually go away. My physiatrist explained that these recurring setbacks could go on for approximately one year from the date of surgery and that people who undergo spine fusion surgery don't recommend the surgery to another patient until about a year after the surgery for this reason. Apparently, it takes approximately that long for the complicated mechanisms in the back to quiet down from the trauma of surgery. Throw in my Crohn's Disease, A+ personality, workaholic nature, and it all was beginning to make medical sense.

Medical reasoning notwithstanding, this setback was not going away and similar to my pre-surgical condition it was causing me such excruciating pain that I couldn't work. At times it was almost like a flashback to my pre-surgery pain - the memories of which I thought I had extinguished with a fair amount of Tequila in Mexico! While my surgeon was courteous, responsive and understanding, he had no medical answers but was confident the pain would pass. My physiatrist, however, was completely perplexed especially given how pain-free I was in almost monthly intervals. I was not a happy camper and was not shy about expressing my dissatisfaction. Part of it was not being able to exercise, part of it was the side effects of the drugs but most of it had to do with my having tasted a pain-free lifestyle and once again being denied access to same.

My high-strung personality, brutal ordeal and need to have results instantaneously, irritated my physicians. I also suspect that my physicians irritated each other. More specifically, the physiatrist at that point was beginning to classify my surgery as a "failed back surgery" and wouldn't render me care unless the surgeon discharged me. My surgeon, however, did not waiver on his aforementioned successful position. This added to the confusion because my physiatrist was the physician who was instrumental in diagnosing my problem and sending me to the appropriate physicians. Now he wouldn't treat me and my surgeon was offering no specific medical guidance other than: "It will pass." As a result, I was actually forced to make a choice between the two doctors because I needed a professional to monitor my treatment, i.e. prescribe drugs, physical therapy, etc. Despite having tremendous confidence in the physiatrist, I couldn't emotionally give in to being treated by a physician who believed the surgical ordeal I went through with my back was all for naught.

BE RESOURCEFUL

Unwilling to give up on the success of my back surgery and receiving no specific medial guidance from my surgeon, I started reading about all sorts of vitamins, herbs and enzymes targeted towards muscle relaxation. I also considered that my body could be having a strange inflammatory response to the surgery. This strange inflammatory response is typical of a patient with an auto-immune illness such as Crohn's Disease. The problem was that my surgeon was a little bit uncomfortable dealing with the muscle pain head-on. Surgeons are like artists. To that extent, they don't deal with picture frames or lighting difficulties. If all looks good on their end, there's nothing more for them to do. With all due respect to my surgeon, he ordered some diagnostic tests and planned to go on more of an offensive approach but waiting was unacceptable to me. As a result, I sought medical advice from a friend of mine who is a prominent local sports medicine physician.

This particular sports medicine physician, who I have known since childhood and who is intensely familiar with my medical background, athletic endeavors and high-strung personality, started me on a regimen of "trigger point" injections (which in all fairness had been recommended by my surgeon). He also put me on a 5-day high dose course of Prednisone (a steroid anti-inflammatory) hoping to reduce the inflammation. I also began wearing copper-magnet bracelets and shoe inserts, took various vitamins and simply prayed that the problem would go away. At the beginning of September, the pain finally disappeared. I kept my surgeon apprised of the treatment all along and he was very supportive. Thereafter, I returned to the pain-free exercise mode and resumed my golfing, weight training and aerobic elliptical exercises.

Since the above initial treatment, I have had slight re-occurrences but thanks to trigger-point injections and small controlled dosages of medications, I have been able to get past these setbacks. However, every time I have twinge of pain or twist the wrong way, I get scared that I am yet again embarking upon another setback.   Now that I have overcome so many, however, I have developed the mental "toughness" to understand that these setbacks are just temporary.   This was a difficult lesson to learn but one that is important to remember when you are recovering from surgery or medical treatment that requires re-strengthening or re-training of the body.

THERE'S NO DRUG PROBLEM – THEY'RE EASY TO GET!

If you have gotten this far in the book, you can probably ascertain that my main objective throughout all my hospital stays is to avoid pain (and of course, Foley Catheters). To do this I have at times become dependent upon narcotic painkillers. This for me is usually the most difficult hurdle to overcome in recuperation. That is, to rid myself of this dependence. In the hospital I am usually either on some sort of intravenous heavy duty pain medication or receive the same via injection. But after a while my treatment slowly gravitates towards my drug of choice that for years has been "Percocet." For those of you who haven't taken this drug, I can only explain it as follows: Not only does it take away the pain, but if you weren't interested in that Buddy Ebsen documentary on the History Channel at 4:00 AM, you will be after taking Percocet. It definitely kills the pain but its euphoric side effect eventually breeds pure desire for the drug. When you start taking the drug for reasons other than pain, you are no longer dependent on the medication but have crossed-over into the unhealthy and dead-end path of addiction. Luckily, I have had excellent doctors who have steered me through these murky waters with precision, compassion and intelligence but it is a battle I have fought for years and will continue to encounter the rest of my life.

My preference for narcotics is probably a byproduct of going to college in the late 1970's/early 1980's. I remember coming home during one Thanksgiving break and sitting at the kitchen table being grilled by my father about stories he had heard concerning widespread drug use in colleges. He eventually asked me point blank if there was a drug problem in school. With a straight face I looked at him and simply stated, "No Dad, there is no drug problem, they're easy to get!" All kidding aside, the physical pain and emotional effects of surgery, the difficulties of the hospital stay and the emotional roller-coaster of recuperation can make a patient cling to a crutch. That crutch is often self-pity, fear and a related dependency on narcotics. Doctors are trained to spot this problem but people with the worst problems are usually the ones who disguise it the best. Take the drugs as long as you need to but be honest with yourself and your doctor as to whether you need or want to take them. If you are in doubt, do without.

The ups and downs of the recuperation process that I endured had me going on and off drugs like Percocet for several months. As such, I experienced "withdrawal" symptoms fairly often. More specifically, the longer you take the narcotic drug, the more likely the chance that the body becomes physically dependent on it. As a result, the body goes through a physical "withdrawal" without it. As the song says, "What Goes Up, Must Come Down." In a hospital setting, this sometimes occurs when doctors discontinue intravenous narcotics such as Morphine or Demerol. If you take such a drug for only a few days after surgery, you probably won't experience much of a withdrawal problem. But if you are in the hospital for days or weeks for medical treatment and require pain medication (as I did at various instances for treatment of my Crohn's Disease), the physical withdrawal symptoms can be stifling.

Besides severe depression, the body's thermostat becomes completely thrown off. As a result, you begin to experience deep chills that are known in medical circles as "goose fever." Sometimes the chills get so intense that you begin to, strangely enough, sweat profusely. Its an incredibly uncomfortable feeling and doesn't make you look too appealing. This is one reason why I closely monitor my pain medication dosages in the hospital because doctors try to get you off of them as quickly as possible. In some instances, it is too quick and the discomfort makes the hospital stay all that more difficult.

Typical withdrawal effects, though, from oral narcotics such as Percocet, are not as severe. However, for 24 to 48 hours after abrupt stoppage of taking the pills, you will experience some depression and goose fever along with diarrhea, cramps and flu-like symptoms. The key to minimizing the withdrawal effects is to gradually reduce the medication so that, for example, each day you take one less pill. But for addictive personalities, this disciplined approach is usually difficult to follow. Speak to your doctor about any concerns and be honest. Doctors don't want to see you in pain but they also do not want you to become addicted to medication.

IT'S ALL RELATIVE

During the recuperation period, try to keep things in perspective. Prior to my back surgery, I was almost suicidal because no one knew what was wrong with me. I logically concluded that if no one could help me I would do something to put an end to my misery because there was no way that I could continue my life in such pain. After the surgery, I was euphoric about my prognosis and future. My business certainly suffered during my ordeal but I made myself a promise that if I were ever to achieve pain-free status I would never again complain about relative trivial matters such as a lost client, poor fiscal quarters, incompetent clerks, botched deals, etc. Of course, I lost sight of this when my back started to feel better and I went back to work.

Whenever I lose perspective on a promise regarding my health (as I did when I resumed working), I go to my local video store and rent the 1978 motion picture, "The End," featuring Burt Reynolds and Dom DeLuise. Reynold's character is a self-centered financially successful real estate type who gets diagnosed with a rare terminal illness and is traumatized when he discovers that no one in his family cares. As a result, he decides to end his life and meets up with DeLuise's character, a maniac, who is more than willing to help him. After several hilarious botched attempts by DeLuise's character to kill him, Reynolds tries to drown himself in the ocean. During this attempt at suicide, Reynolds suddenly discovers his will to live. The problem is that he has drifted so far out in the ocean that without divine intervention he ironically will die.

As a last resort, he appeals to the heavens and says: "Help me make it and I'll give you 50% of everything I make! 50%, God! I want to point out, God, that nobody gives 50%! I'm talking 'gross' God!" Almost immediately after this promise he somehow finds the strength to battle the tide and swim to shore. Feeling rejuvenated and blessed as he gets closer to shore and realizing he will not drown, Reynolds looks up at the sky, thanks

God and says: "I'm gonna start donating that 10% right away. I know I said 50%, Lord - but 10% to start. If you don't want your 10% - then don't take it! I know it was you who saved me but it was also you that made me sick!"

In a real funny way that scene reminds me not to forget my promise. For at least a few days after I watch it, I don't take for granted what truly is important, that is, my health. If you have your health, well, you're lucky. If you don't and you get it back, you're even luckier. Be grateful and keep things in perspective because by comparison things can always be worse. Once you realize that, things usually get better.

Chapter 9

APPEALING MANAGED CARE COVERAGE DECISIONS

DAMN THE TORPEDOS

Good luck! This, by far, is the most agonizing aspect of the hospital stay. It can make even my Foley Catheter experience seem pleasurable by comparison! Okay, that's a slight exaggeration but the process is brutal. It's much more manageable if you follow my instructions in Chapter 1 regarding the purchasing of a computer/scanner to organize all medical referrals, receipts and declination letters because it seems as if the people reviewing claims automatically deny coverage the first thirty-seven times the claims are submitted. Some examiners do not even send declination letters. They just ignore the claims. When you call to inquire, they blame the foul-up on having never received the claim. If you then try to speak to a supervisor you are in for what could be "A Three Hour Tour, A Three Hour Tour." Others send the declination letters only to the providers thus depriving you of an opportunity to timely and discreetly make certain that the insurer is providing the coverage for which you are paying.

WHEN THE BALANCE
OF POWER SHIFTS

I sincerely believe these claim examiners are compassionate individuals because after all they are patients, parents, grandparents, etc. They are just overwhelmed by the paperwork. Therefore, it's best to be pleasant and play along because initially the insurance company holds and yields all the power. However, once they put a claim decision in writing, whether it is an approval or denial, you must exercise your right to appeal it if you are dissatisfied because that is when the balance of power shifts. More specifically, upon purchasing your health insurance coverage you agreed to some form of dispute resolution process that grants you the right to contest a coverage decision. The details of this process are usually in small print and contained in a separate part of your agreement. Typically, the process involves the binding authority of a "Grievance Appeal Committee" as the final arbiter of your fate. However, there is case law in several states and pending federal legislation that suggest health insurance companies can nevertheless be sued for various coverage and declination decisions.

This chapter details the process I underwent in successfully seeking resolution for reimbursement of approximately $12,000 worth of diagnostic tests for which I was denied coverage by my insurance carrier on at least five occasions. I experienced the balance of power shift first-hand luckily without having to go to court. Every insurance company is operated differently but claims processing and the related appeal mechanisms are usually the same. Therefore, hopefully you can benefit from my experience. For reference purposes, Appendix C contains most of the actual correspondences (they are organized in chronological order with the most current at the beginning) that were exchanged during the process. The reminder of the correspondences, such as several declination letters, were sent directly to the providers involved. I was notified of their existence through telephone conversations with various provider office staff members.

THE REJECTED DISCOGRAMS

As I made reference in Chapter 4 while explaining the "Business Letter," prior to my back surgery I was forced to seek medical care outside of my health insurance "network" for diagnostic tests. By way of background, the cause of my pain was not revealing itself on all conventional testing such as x-rays, MRIs, Cat Scans, EMGs and Bone Scans. Thankfully, my physiatrist, who was overseeing my lack of progress in physical therapy, thought my problem emanated from "Degenerative Disc Disease." To confirm this diagnosis, he recommended that I undergo a "discogram." As it was explained to me, this is a surgical-like procedure performed by surgeons and certain physiatrists in which saline is injected directly into the suspected disc and radiographic images of the disc's reaction are simultaneously captured under fluoroscopy (i.e. taking x-ray/cat scan images).

The diagnostic theory is simple. The disc is supposed to hold a certain amount of fluid. If after being injected with this fluid the disc leaks or ruptures, it is clear there is a disc problem. Usually the problem becomes immediately apparent to the physician during the test. However, in certain instances, the tear or rupture in the disc is so deep that it will not leak fluid. Such an abnormality though will reveal itself in the radiographic images. More importantly, the doctor should recreate the patient's pain because the degenerated or ruptured disc does not take too kindly to being stuck with needles and shot up with excessive amounts of fluid. To that extent, the doctor also relies on the patient's response during the test to pinpoint the area of concern. As a result, no anesthesia is used during the procedure.

"REASONABLE & CUSTOMARY"

I thought it would be easy to obtain a referral for the discogram to be performed by a physician in my insurance company's "network" since it was a doctor in the network, namely my physiatrist, who recommended the test. However, the surgeon I was referred to for a consultation would not perform the discogram because there were no positive findings on my other diagnostic tests. Given my symptoms, failed physical therapy, numerous epidural injections and dependence on large doses of narcotic painkillers, this was precisely the reason why he should have performed the discogram. My insurance company permitted me to go outside of the physician network but such "out-of-network" reimbursement would only be 80% of what it deemed to be the "reasonable and customary" charge for such a service.

My friends never seem to understand how such a formula can result in such substantial debt since the remaining 20% "can't possibly amount to a great deal of money." The catch is the language "reasonable and customary." More specifically, insurance companies assess a certain value to a particular service provided regardless of where it is rendered (e.g. New York City vs. a rural suburb of Montana) or what dollar amount the patient is billed. The insurance company then reimburses the patient, or pays the provider, 80% of the assessed figure. For example, if I were charged $6,000 dollars for the discogram, my insurer might conclude that the reasonable and customary charge for the procedure is $3,200 and then pay the provider 80% of it or a total of $2,560. The provider would then "balance bill" me $3,440. To me, that's "a great deal of money."

113

GET PROOF THAT YOU FOLLOWED, OR TRIED TO FOLLOW, ALL REQUIRED NETWORK AND REFERRAL RULES

Acutely aware of the possible financial ramifications, I diligently attempted to find a surgeon or physiatrist in my network to perform the discogram. Of course, I first had to get a referral from my primary care physician or gatekeeper. He was compassionate about my plight and sincerely wanted to see me pain-free but because the specialist he referred me to (the "Business Letter" doctor) would not perform the discogram, he apparently couldn't then go ahead and recommend I have the test performed by another specialist in the network. This made no sense because he had also referred me to the physiatrist who recommended that I undergo the discogram. I suspect this illogical situation was a by-product of what are probably unwritten but mutually understood and enforced referral rules among fellow physician network members.

I knew at that point that I would be getting the test "out-of-network" but I had to obtain some proof that doctors in the network wouldn't perform the test. I also had no patience for the politics involved because I knew my failure to follow the network/referral rules would be used against me in an appeal regardless of the reason. I explained this to my primary care physician's office manager and she somehow managed to get the gatekeeper to sign off on a referral. The logic of the situation made sense to her so she did everything she could to help me including the provision of names of doctors in the network who she thought might perform the test. We both knew they wouldn't perform the test on me but the fact they performed the test combined with the written referral was all I needed.

I called approximately ten of these doctors but none would perform the test either because they were unavailable or because they didn't see a need for it given that all my other tests were negative. Each time I hung up the phone I felt as if I had wandered into the "Saturday Night Live" Greek Diner skit with John Belushi where despite whatever a customer orders he receives a cheeseburger. I'd ask for a discogram, and they'd each say "Have you tried physical therapy?" These doctors were not listening to me and that was incredibly frustrating since I had been discharged from a local hospital 24 hours earlier in a condition necessitating large amounts of narcotics simply to walk.

EVALUATING THE COST OF GOING "OUT-OF-NETWORK"

I knew of a well-known doctor in New York City who would perform the test but he was "out-of-network" and I was afraid that not only would my insurance company pay only 80% of its reasonable and customary determination of his fee but it might deny reimbursement completely if it deemed the test "not medically necessary." That likelihood was high since each "network" specialist had declined to perform the discogram and I had trouble simply getting the referral from my gatekeeper. If the service was deemed "not medically necessary," my insurance company would pay nothing. To make matters worse, the New York City doctor performed the test at a hospital that was also out-of-network. As there would undoubtedly be hospital charges associated with the test (such as supplies, radiographic equipment, technicians and nurses), the total out-of-network cost appeared staggering.

I had no choice but to go into New York City and undergo the test. Luckily, the test proved positive results at the L5-S1 disc level. However, after viewing the results, the doctor felt it was necessary to perform another discogram to rule out abnormalities in any other levels so that if surgery was the option a surgeon would know exactly what to fix and where. Given that back problems are highly complicated and the pain could be deceptive, I went for the other discogram because I was fearful of an unnecessary or unsuccessful back surgery. The results on the other levels proved negative and the surgical area was pinpointed. Eventually, as you know by now, I had the surgery approximately a month and a half after the discograms. The month and a half time lag was due to the surgeon selection process which was an equally frustrating experience and is somewhat addressed in Chapter 4's "Fighting Back Letter."

PREPARING FOR BATTLE

I submitted to my insurance company the bills for the two (2) discograms in the approximate amount of $12,000 which included the hospital's charges. However, I included a detailed letter (see November 20, 1998 letter in Appendix C) to lay the proper foundation for an appeal as I knew one would be necessary. I then underwent my surgery and forgot about it until I was sufficiently recuperated from the surgery to deal with the financial aftermath. I tried to cover every base by obtaining "medically necessary" letters from both the physician who performed the discogram (see November 23, 1998 letter in Appendix C) and my surgeon (see June 23, 1999 letter in Appendix C). My surgeon was kind enough to add in that he operated on me primarily because of the results of the discograms.

I figured based upon my explanation for the need of the test and the subsequent successful surgery, the insurance company would see the light and pay these bills as if they were rendered "in-network." After reviewing my policy, I knew the insurance company was required to pay for services that were medically necessary so long as I used the in-network physicians. If I could prove the discograms were medically necessary and I was denied an opportunity to have them performed by an in-network physician, the insurance company would legally have to treat the tests as having been performed in-network. As such, each test would then cost me $15.00. Now, that is not a great deal of money. Nevertheless, I kept getting rejection letters from the insurance company and notices of same from both the physician and the hospital.

A STOP-GAP MEASURE

During this process, I was extremely sensitive about my obligation to the physician who performed the discograms because he rendered an extremely valuable service to me at a time when no one else would. However, I did not have the money to pay him since my business was in complete disarray because I hadn't been able to work since July of 1998 and would be out of work until approximately June of 1999. As a preemptive gesture, I sent him a check for $500 as a good faith payment towards my bill. I also enclosed a letter with my check that stated that I fully intended to honor the bill even if it meant paying it out over the rest of my life. However, I also indicated that I was engaging in an appeal process with my insurance company and would sincerely appreciate if he would be patient because I thought I had a strong case. I didn't keep a copy of the letter because it was painful to write and depressing to look at. Luckily, this doctor was as honorable as I'd like to think I am and he agreed. I think he also saw the merits of my case and was willing to give me the benefit of the doubt.

DAMN THE TORPEDOES

After receiving several rejection letters and developing an ulcer, I opted to test the binding Grievance Appeal Committee ("Committee") mechanism in my insurance plan. I was notified that it would be an informal proceeding and that I could obtain legal counsel if I preferred (see the "Grievance Appeal Committee Rules" attached to the July 7, 1999 letter in Appendix C). I called and inquired about additional formalities but didn't receive much information. All I was told was that it was only necessary to attend if I had anything additional for the Committee to consider. I had sent every possible communication as an exhibit in my previous correspondences so there technically was nothing additional to add to my presentation. However, being trained as an attorney I am extremely passionate about a client and his/her concerns, particularly if that client is me and the concerns involve $12,000! There was no way I wasn't attending.

THE GRIEVANCE APPEAL HEARING

I was told to arrive at the local corporate offices of my insurance company at a specific time and that I would have approximately a thirty minute hearing. I was cautioned to be brief because the "subscriber" appeals were staggered in thirty-minute intervals throughout the day. When I arrived at the plush corporate offices, I was eventually lead up to a conference room that was as intimidating as any corporate boardroom I had been in as practicing attorney. After I sat down, the insurance company's legal counsel explained that the three individuals sitting across from me would decide my fate. Each individual was then introduced "on the record" for the benefit of a stenographer.

One Committee member was an insurance company physician, another was an insurance company subscriber like myself and the other was an insurance company employee whose job duties were unrelated to the determination of health insurance claims. None of the individuals were involved in my case but each had received all my correspondences and supposedly reviewed same prior to the hearing. Even with my experience as an attorney, this was an intimidating atmosphere because there was a great deal of money at stake and I was "playing on the road" before a hostile crowd. That home court advantage grew exponentially when immediately before officially commencing the proceeding approximately ten (10) supposedly disinterested insurance company employees were led into the conference room.

Even with the ten additional individuals, there was room to spare in this huge corporate boardroom. However, I was more concerned with the insurance company's apparent attempt at intimidating me by filling the room with ten insurance company employees under the pretext of observing the process. It reminded me of the scene in the motion picture, "The Godfather," when Michael Corleone flew in Frankie Pentangeli's brother from Sicily under the guise of showing sibling support in the courtroom. "Don" Corleone was actually telling Pentangeli that his brother would be killed if his testimony was damaging to the "Family."

I suddenly was inspired by the insurance company's arrogance. However, I couldn't reveal my concern because I didn't want to come across as a typical lawyer looking for some sort of technicality to win a case. Nevertheless, I knew I had to address the situation because it simply wasn't fair. To that extent, I went "on the record" and explained that while I am an attorney I do not intend to use my skills in this matter because this is not a legal proceeding. But, in the interest of fairness, I was somewhat concerned by the additional people paraded into the room and would appreciate if each would go on the record and introduce themselves and briefly describe the nature of their position with the insurance company.

This was a fine line to walk because I didn't want my legal skills to alienate the two Committee members I knew would be on my side once they heard the facts. I had no prayer with the doctor and just planned on controlling my prejudice towards him. Actually, he seemed like a nice individual. I just wasn't a big fan of my insurance company's "network" physicians at the time. As each of the ten employees proceeded up to the microphone and described their respective jobs, I watched my two Committee members begin to feel sorry for me. I sat and smiled throughout all the introductions and marveled at the increasing comprehensive disastrous effect of the insurance company's arrogance for having tried to intimidate me.

MY PRESENTATION

As soon as the Head of Janitorial Services had finished introducing the four or five members of his staff who had come to attend the hearing on an "observation basis," I began my presentation. The insurance company's legal counsel had asked me only to address additional information but I ignored her remark because the insurance company had trounced on my rights at every opportunity. I tried to get the Committee to view me as a person and not just an insurance company subscriber. I was careful to explain the discogram procedure in layman terms so that my two Committee members related to it but I included a fair amount of specificity so that the doctor on the panel did not feel that I was patronizing him. I was also careful to praise the insurance company for its prompt response in other aspects of my back surgery. That may have been patronizing but I was patronizing a company and not a person so I saw nothing wrong with my approach.

GET A LAWYER

After my presentation, the doctor asked me several questions. His overall strategy was to dehumanize me and my suffering. However, he disguised his approach with specific questions about my diligence to seek "in-network" provision of the discograms. It was very interesting because he was trying to get me to say something that would indicate that I went "out-of-network" without first trying to obtain these services "in-network." As I detailed above, I did make an earnest effort at trying to get the test "in-network" but unfortunately I had no substantial proof of my phone conversations with these various physicians and/or their office managers. I should have documented these conversations but my physical and mental condition was so fragile that getting treatment and not documenting refusals of treatment was my primary concern.

My lack of proof notwithstanding, the doctor was ineffective because he was in my arena as this was a legal proceeding despite disclaimers to the contrary. My description of my ordeal made an indelible impression upon my two Committee members. I also was careful to stand during my presentation and demonstrate how healthy I was as a result of the surgery. This further demonstrated the medical necessity of the discograms. For $12,000, I would have tap-danced naked if I had to! I felt confident at the end of the questioning and declined to add any additional information resting on the extensive written information I had submitted and my presentation up until that point. Within a few days I received the Committee's letter (see August 25, 1999 letter in Appendix C) indicating that my appeal was successful.

WHAT CAN YOU DO?

The appeal process with my insurance company took a long time and a tremendous amount of effort on my part but in the end justice prevailed. Sometimes, I have seen my insurance company reverse a claim decision simply based upon an identical re-submission of the claim. Other times, however, I don't think hiring Johnnie Cochran would have made a difference. So what can you do? The first step, and the overall strategy, is to humanize the claim.

If you are too emotional, frustrated or ill-equipped to contend with the seemingly never ending letter writing, claim submissions and overall paperwork battles, consider hiring either an attorney or a "Patient Advocate" to represent your interests. At the paperwork stage, a lawyer might be a bit of a luxury. However, a "Patient Advocate" or "Claim Filing Consultant" could be the answer. I have never had to hire one because of my training as an attorney. However, I understand the need for this type of assistance is creating a growing industry of professionals. The need for these services is becoming so pervasive that it is likely you will find listings in your local telephone directories. However, I suggest that before you engage the services of such a professional you ask for names of three clients as references to verify that they are competent, reputable and results-oriented. The Internet is a good place to start in your research for a competent professional in this area. While I am sure there are many organizations dedicated to these types of problems, the one I am somewhat familiar with is the Alliance of Claims Assistance Professionals ("ACAP") whose mission statement on its Web site (www.claims.org) is: "Professionals dedicated to the effective management of health insurance claims." I have never used their services but I am certainly impressed with their intentions.

Above all else, be persistent and disregard all declination letters because for all you know they were automatically generated by a computer. Also, be exacting in your correspondences and keep accurate records detailing phone calls and voice-mail messages sent and received. Accuracy and good record keeping are the best defense against incompetence, stupidity and breach of contract. Finally, don't lose sight of the fact that insurance companies are not looking to exploit sick people in need of quality medical care. They are merely seeking to weed out false claims or claims by lazy individuals who refuse to follow the rules to which they agreed regarding the delivery of their medical care. Once you convince the insurance company that you are not one of those individuals, you will have greatly enhanced your chances for reimbursement of your claim.

Chapter 10

FOR WHAT IT'S WORTH

HUMBLE SUGGESTIONS

You just found out you need surgery. The surgeon you prefer operates at a hospital in which you had a bad experience. Another surgeon can competently perform the operation at your preferred hospital, but she is slightly less qualified than your preferred surgeon. Without question, you will choose the surgeon over the hospital because the quality of care delivered in the hospital is secondary to the quality of the physician delivering the care. Now the "SAT" type question - what if the choice is between two exactly comparable surgeons both in your HMO but each operates at vastly different quality level hospitals and the poorer quality hospital is in your HMO and the other is not? Without question, you will choose the surgeon in the HMO hospital because the quality of care delivered in the hospital is also secondary to the cost of hospitalization.

CREATE A MORE PATIENT-FRIENDLY ATMOSPHERE

I do not believe hospital patient care needs radical improvement because for the most part hospitals provide excellent care. But is there even an incentive for hospitals to address the quality of the patient experience? No. As long as patients are influenced strictly by physician selection and cost, hospitals needn't be concerned. I just wish they would be because just a few innovative, inexpensive efforts would yield exponential positive results. More specifically, I suggest that hospitals focus a bit more on re-educating medical professionals about the patient experience and strive toward creating a more "patient friendly" atmosphere.

Prior to entering law school, I never had an interaction with an attorney. I met people who were attorneys but never required the services of one. I didn't even know people who hired attorneys. Nonetheless, I dedicated three years of my life and thousands of dollars to study law and become an attorney. It was "blind" ambition as I had no idea about what I was getting into. The television show "LA Law" made it seem glamorous, but nothing I had experienced prepared me for the day-to-day grind and interaction with clients. Medical professionals are not so disadvantaged because regardless of their title or specialty they are in the business of treating patients and every person has been a patient. Not everyone has been a hospital patient, but all human beings have experienced the vulnerability and insecurity of being sick and in need of medical care. Yet, despite the perspective of this "20/20" foresight, some medical professionals in hospitals often behave as if they are completely unfamiliar with the patient experience. It is this infrequent but significant perceived ignorance of patient issues, concerns and fears that sometimes makes being a hospital patient an unpleasant experience.

BECOME MORE FAMILIAR
WITH THE PATIENT EXPERIENCE

As detailed throughout this book, medical professionals have difficult jobs and demanding customers. To that extent, I understand the occasional lapse in appreciation of the patient experience. However, based upon my experience, the most effective hospital physicians, nurses and therapists are the ones most closely in touch with the patient experience. Not only do they understand this essential element in effective treatment but they also seem to appreciate that they are possibly one infection away from hospitalization. This understanding and appreciation should be taught to those professionals who for whatever reason have forgotten that they are treating people not symptoms. They would then think twice before summarily dismissing certain patients and their concerns.

EMPHASIZE PATIENT "CARE" OVER PATIENT "COST"

While the personalities and perspectives of a few hospital personnel can make the hospital stay difficult, the increasingly prevalent de-humanizing hospital atmosphere makes optimally effective hospital treatment nearly impossible. With the advent of managed care and rapid technological advancements, hospitals are no longer "patient friendly." The emphasis is increasingly on patient "cost" rather than patient "care." While these structural and technological advancements have made health care more accessible to the masses and lengthened lives, they have also unnecessarily created an often unfriendly and "bottom-line" atmosphere. Unfortunately, I believe this atmosphere has affected both the quality and delivery of care. Advancement need not breed arrogance or de-humanization. After all, the corporate organizations that have created the most technology are also the same ones that have introduced a more laid-back or personal approach to business.

SATISFIED PATIENTS
SHOULD BE THE STANDARD

With the proliferation of "Dress Down" days, flex-time schedules, home/office workers, corporate daycare and virtual offices, these successful corporate organizations simultaneously reward individualization and people skills while maintaining their bottom-line focus. Creativity and "user friendly" approaches are now the norm and not the exception because the corporate world has concluded that employees and customers must be treated the same because people are the most important resource and their satisfaction alone is what ultimately determines success. Isn't that true of hospital patients? Sure, hospital physicians and nurses should be well compensated but isn't the quality of their work and thus their value determined by the satisfaction of the patients? The last thing we need is companies like Microsoft or Dell Computer owning and operating hospitals, but hospitals could learn a great deal from their successful approach.

IMPLEMENT INNOVATIVE
SLEEPOVER PROGRAMS

Before a complete corporate makeover, however, hospitals and medical schools should hire people like myself to share patient perspectives with their employees and students to insure that their practices and training techniques are "patient friendly." If possible they should go one step further and require hospital professionals, including, but not limited to, physicians, nurses, administrators, occupational therapists, office managers, patient representatives and even orderlies to be confined as hospital patients for a period of time long enough to simulate the patient experience. It will have been long enough if they experience the vulnerability, frustration, isolation and fear associated with being a hospital patient. Practicality may severely limit the length of confinement but the hospitalization should include at least two (2) consecutive overnight stays. As each is involved in selling the hospital's service and in essence must convince the patient-customer to come back the next time they need hospital services, shouldn't they have an understanding and appreciation of the needs and desires of the customer? Wouldn't that acquired perspective make a strong but subtle sales pitch? Maybe then a hospital's quality of service will make a difference in patient preferences. Wouldn't the hospital then benefit?

In the event practicality precludes such an innovative program, it might be a good idea for medical school students and hospital personnel to watch the motion picture, "The Doctor," starring William Hurt. It is a dramatic example of an arrogant physician who changes his demeanor because of his experiences as a patient after he is forced to undergo rigorous chemotherapy treatments. His physical and emotional feelings humble him and make him more sensitive to patient vulnerabilities, frustrations and fears. In the end, he becomes a better doctor, husband, father and human being. All medical professionals are not like the self-important William Hurt character. In fact, most are sympathetic, kind, warm and compassionate individuals. However, the effect their jobs have on people's lives creates a normal proclivity for arrogant and condescending behavior. I'm just suggesting that this tendency be addressed because its mere acknowledgement would greatly enhance the hospital patient experience.

<u>PROMOTE NORMALCY - UTILIZE</u> <u>CELEBRITIES</u>

Many celebrities donate their time and money to hospitals and medical related charitable organizations. Often, they visit hospitalized children in an attempt to raise their hopes. While some of the visits are genuine, the inherent impersonal aspect of the celebrity "visit experience" suggests that many could be for public relations purposes. Celebrities who really care, however, understand that making a difference requires a solid long-term commitment - whether that is personal appearances or financial contributions. To that extent, I believe the most effective way for celebrities to make a difference is to help make hospitals "patient friendly." More specifically, they can help fund computer lounges where children can interact on the Internet. They can also help fund, and participate in, lecture bureaus that stimulate adult patients with interesting and motivational speakers on topics such as computers, financial planning, travel, sports, etc. The key is to promote normal life activities inside the hospital so that patients view the hospital as nothing more and nothing less than what it has to be, i.e., a professional place to go for medical treatment.

Once the normalcy from a patient's life is interrupted, the patient will begin viewing the hospital stay as confinement and will therefore begin focusing on his/her illness and the inadequacies of the hospital and/or its healthcare workers. If celebrities can make milk look cool, imagine what they can do for the potential innovative recreational activities inside the hospital? This "normalcy" strategy will become increasingly important as more devastating illnesses are cured and treatment requires patients to become even more dependent than ever on hospitals. For example, some patients now obtain life-saving drug infusion treatments at their local hospital during their lunch hour for once thought to be terminal illnesses.

Patients do not stop being people once they put on the hospital wristband. More importantly, just because an individual is a patient doesn't mean he or she ceases being a husband, wife, grandmother, son, daughter, employee, friend etc. Medical professionals need to realize this and incorporate the patient/people perspective in designing the atmosphere and operation of the hospital. As in all causes that impact the masses, celebrity participation would greatly enhance the success and development of such ideas.

ACKNOWLEDGEMENTS

My parents may not have passed on the healthiest genes, but they showed me how to laugh and taught me how to cope with, and learn from, adversity. While this is the part of the book where I should be sentimental, I'm not gonna lie - I would have preferred that they taught me how to play polo or become an expert yacht racer! In all seriousness, my parents' success with me is demonstrated in the remarkable friendships I have established, maintained and treasured. I would go through each and every experience, emotion and physical malady that is detailed in this book just on the promise that these friendships would be there for me in the end. I didn't inherit my coping abilities because these skills and personality traits are not "passed down" from one generation to the next. I acquired them by watching and observing the examples set by my parents.

My mother, Bernice Weiss, is by far the most competent, confident, fearless and positive person I have met in my life. There has been no obstacle too big to stop her from helping me get the medical attention and personal happiness she thought I required or deserved. Since sports metaphors, particularly those related to baseball, help me make sense of things when words don't, I can best describe my acknowledgement of my Mom's contributions by making her the Number 3 hitter in the batting order of my own "Team of Support." Whenever I've needed a hit she got it, or if she didn't, she fouled off about 20 tough pitches and set up the next batter to come through for me. Much like Keith Hernandez of the 1986 New York Mets, she's also been the anchor on the field, the leader in the clubhouse and can best be described as dependable, reliable and dedicated. Thus, when she encouraged me to write this book, I listened.

Many parents teach children with the philosophy of: "Do as I say, not as I do." This has not been the style of my father, Jerry Weiss, when it has come to me and my becoming a man. I watched him battle cancer, life-threatening heart and lung problems, disabling and crippling injuries (including the manufacturer recall of an artificial knee!) with stoic pride, quiet class and self-deprecating humor. I am sure behind closed doors at times he cried and struggled with these problems but I never saw him once question his then-apparent fate or curse his predicament. He faced these obstacles while raising three children and starting his own successful business and yet, now at the age of 69, if you ask him, he will tell you he has had a wonderful life. My mother and his grandchildren are the primary reason for his happiness but he is solely responsible for surviving. He never told me how tough he was, or how tough I should be, he just showed me. I owe my unique perspective and resiliency to my father for imparting this invaluable wisdom to me. This book is a celebration of that wisdom and therefore a salute to my father. He would be the "Clean-up" or No. 4 hitter in my line-up.

Leading off (batting first) is either one of my four nephews, Robbie Toll (14 years old), Brian Toll (11), Adam Seldon (14) or Corey Seldon (11). Each in their own way has always made me feel vibrant and important despite the circumstance or my condition at the time. Each has a unique blend of sensitivity, athleticism and toughness that reminds me of myself. They have also shown tremendous interest in this book which is quite amazing considering their ages and that they seem to only get excited about NFL Football, Professional Wrestling, Pamela Anderson and Puff Daddy! I guess you could say that much like certain Hall-of-Fame lead-off hitter, Ricky Henderson, they each have that special blend of speed, smarts and power.

Batting second is either one of my four (4) siblings, namely, my sisters Mindy Seldon, Eileen Toll and their respective husbands, Richard and Jimmy. Each in his or her own way has always been able to "move the runner over" and also "hit one into the gap" if necessary. Mindy, though, has added unparalleled warmth, humor and hope to my life particularly at times when I doubted my ability or desire to keep on coping.

This despite her being the queen of "Don't worry, it can't get any worse" when it always does! One day, this consistent but hopelessly funny dialogue between us regarding her well-intentioned advice and my bad luck gave me the idea to share my ridiculous and never-ending medical experiences with other patients. Thanks, Min, I finally saw the humor in it and the result was this book.

While out of batting line-up order and slightly out of sequence with the baseball metaphor, my two Aunt and Uncles, Joan/Max and Mary/David, comprise my coaching staff along with a former professor of mine, Abraham Stein. "Dr." Stein's wisdom has always helped me focus on what is important despite the challenges and difficulties at hand. He was the first to give me the confidence to "put pen to paper" about anything in which I believed. Despite possessing senses of humor and understanding so pure people can't help but be drawn to him, my Uncle Maxie may be the only patient who irritates doctors more than myself. He's a good example of how difficult it is being a hospital patient and was in my thoughts when I wrote most of this book. My Aunt Joanie has had her own recent battles with the hospital system but amazingly never even flinched. Her quiet strength and enthusiastic support of my efforts regarding this book were inspiring and sincerely appreciated. Besides always providing expert moral support throughout my ordeals, my Uncle David was responsible for the corned beef sandwich in Chapter 5 which in retrospect helped spark my interest in writing that chapter.

My "Team of Support" Manager is Dr. Mark Chapman, my gastroenterologist and Brian Dennehy look-a-like who has been the most comprehensive, up-to-date, intelligent, resourceful, and compassionate physician I have ever encountered. His staff, Lynn, Sandy, Nancy and various other individuals have listened to my problems and expertly facilitated my care for the past seventeen years. In many ways, they and their counterparts taught me how to be a patient and have respect for those in more urgent need of medical attention. Dr. Chapman is rather humble and as a result I refrained from using his name in the book. However, anytime I was required to investigate surgical options, invasive procedures, begin new medications or experienced any sort of complication regardless of how bizarre, he was the professional who supplied the answer. He either dealt with the situation directly or maneuvered behind the scenes to make sure my concerns were addressed to my satisfaction. Above all else though, no matter how ill I am, I feel better the instant I hear his voice.

Lloyd Litwak and Richard Kenyon would be my No. 5 hitters as each have provided emotional and financial support for any endeavor, problem or encounter I have ever experienced. They always offered to help me at their own initiative and have never made me feel uncomfortable having to ask for their support. I know we can't choose our relatives but if I could have brothers, these two guys would be them. Although Lloyd can't hit a curve ball (despite his stories of Little League success to the contrary) and Rich has become such a good golfer (?) that he no longer can handle high "heat," I'd feel confident having them back up my father in the No. 5 slot. Both Rich and Lloyd, perhaps the least likely individuals to be interested in a book on the hospital patient experience, read the initial draft and provided solid encouragement. That was important to me and opened my eyes to the book's potential significance to the general public.

Equally as important, but in different ways, Elana Cooper, Sandy and Rona Nelson, Bruce and Paula Nyfield, Steven and Kim Brier, Eric and Nicole Dorsky, Matthew and Lori Lustig, Barry Brandt, Harris and Dahna Freidus and Dennis and Sylvana Cardone would round out the batting order. Each in their own way have encouraged me in my pursuits, made me proud of their own personal choices and most of all made me laugh. Accounts of their hospital visits, telephone calls and rehabilitation support are sprinkled in throughout the book. These are the kind of friends who know what you are thinking before you say it, make you feel comfortable when you come to visit, genuinely take interest in your life and really care about your well-being. Each has also accomplished a tremendous amount in their lives and has made me proud to call them my friends and confidantes. To refer to any of them as No. 6, 7, 8 or 9 hitters is a bit of an insult but I got quite a squad and each has at one time or another skillfully taken over the 3, 4 and 5 spots in the order. They each have also provided me with solid encouragement regarding this book including taking the time to read the various drafts, revisions and to comment on same.

My batting order would not be complete if I didn't write-in Jennifer Coleman as the designated hitter. Jennifer served as my assistant/secretary during the incredibly trying times involving the diagnosis and treatment of my back problem and was adamant that I finish this book. Although I wish Jennifer had a lead foot while driving (see Chapter 7), the day I hired her as my assistant was the day my law practice began to thrive. She will never grasp the concept of the "apostrophe," but she believed in this book from the beginning and motivated me to complete it.

The starting pitchers in my line-up are the various physicians who have taken significant roles in my life by helping me use my scarred body to keep the promises of my hyperactive mind. They each possess a combination of skill, respectful demeanor, compassion and interest that is hard to find in the health care industry. These doctors, in no particular order of their contributions, are as follows: Andrew Casden, Joel Bauer, the late, but great, Irwin Gelent, Howard Berg, Vivek Das, Gregory Lutz, Brian Halpern, James Petros, Gerard Malanga, Glen Mogan, Peter Banks, John Russo, Bill Nadelberg, some of their respective covering physicians and all of their office staff support people (thanks Roseanne). I also owe a great debt of gratitude to the numerous emergency room physicians and technicians throughout the country whose nights I complicated, ruined or made difficult. They were kind, compassionate and patient despite my complicated medical condition and probably difficult mental state.

Other individuals who have been supportive of my plight and shown tremendous interest in the development and completion of this book are the following: my cousins Jill and Jeff Strauss, Jeffrey and Nancy Weiss and Michelle and Evan Moretzsky; Tina Eichenholz; Robert Fuld; Suzanne Kimel; Lisa Reifer-Cohen; Regina McGuire; George Veras; Alisa Arnoff; Lloyd Jassin, Esq., Todd Brower and Wendy Granberg. I also sincerely appreciate the support and encouragement of all the friends and acquaintances I've met along the way who visited and/or called me during my numerous hospital stays. Their concern and support contributed greatly to the conception and development of the book. Kudos also to the people I didn't know quite as well who read the first draft and took the time to constructively comment upon the style, idea and prospect of success. The mere fact that they took a few hours of their time to read about my patient experiences provided empowering inspiration that fueled my desire to finish the book (Thank You Lou Wolfe). The happy ending, by the way, has in large part been brought to you by the excellent work of my physical therapists - thanks Jeannie, Christian and Rodney.

I am also grateful to all the hospital nurses, orderlies, patient representatives and other health care workers who over the years treated me with dignity, compassion, respect and complete professionalism. Last, but certainly not least, I applaud the existence, development and importance of the Crohn's & Colitis Foundation of America ("CCFA") and will remain forever grateful to the past, present and future CCFA individuals responsible for making life normal with Crohn's Disease.

January 2001

APPENDIX "A"

<u>SAMPLE</u> LIVING WILL

ADVANCE DIRECTIVE FOR HEALTH CARE

("LIVING WILL")

FOR

_____

I understand that as a competent adult I have the right to make decisions about my health care. There may come a time when I am unable, due to physical or mental incapacity, to make my own health care decisions. In these circumstances, those caring for me will need direction concerning my care and will turn to someone who knows my values and health care wishes. I understand that those responsible for my care will seek to make health care decisions in my best interests, based upon what they know of my wishes. In order to provide the guidance and authority needed to make decisions on my behalf:

I, _____, hereby declare and make known my instructions and wishes for my future care. This advance directive for health care shall take effect in the event I become unable to make my own health care decisions, as determined by the physician who has primary responsibility for my care, and any necessary confirming determinations. I direct that this document become part of my permanent medical records.

A. <u>CHOOSING A HEALTH CARE REPRESENTATIVE</u>:

I hereby designate:

Name:

Address:

Phone:

Email:

as my Health Care Representative ("Agent") to make all health care decisions for me, including decisions to accept or refuse any treatment, service or procedure used to diagnose or treat my physical or mental condition, and decisions to provide, withhold or withdraw life-sustaining measures. I direct my Agent to make decisions on my behalf in accordance with my wishes as stated in this document, or as otherwise known to him. In the event my wishes are not clear, or a situation arises I did not anticipate, my health care representative is authorized to make decisions in my best interests, based upon what is known of my wishes.

I have discussed the terms of this designation with my Agent and he has willingly agreed to accept the responsibility for acting on my behalf.

B. <u>ALTERNATIVE AGENTS</u>:

If the person I have designated above is unable, unwilling or unavailable to act as my agent, I hereby designate the following person(s) to act as my health care representative, in the order of priority stated:

1.

2.

C. AUTHORITY OF AGENT:

My Agent is authorized to make any and all health care decisions for me that may be deemed appropriate by my Agent, subject to my wishes and the limitations (if any) as stated in this document. My Agent shall request and evaluate information concerning my medical diagnosis, the prognosis, the benefits and risks of the proposed health care, and alternatives to the proposed health care. My Agent shall consider the decision that I would have made if I had the ability to do so. If my Agent does not know my wishes regarding a specific health care decision, my Agent shall make a decision for me in accordance with what my Agent determines to be in my best interest. In determining my best interest, my Agent shall consider my personal beliefs and basic values to the extent known to my Agent.

My Agent must try to discuss health care decisions with me. However, if I am unable to communicate, my Agent may make such decisions for me.

To that extent deemed appropriate by my Agent, my Agent may discuss health care decisions with my family and others, to the extent they are available.

I authorize my Agent to:

a. Request, receive and review any information, verbal or written, regarding my physical or mental health including medical and hospital records, and to consent to the disclosure of such records to others.
b. Execute on my behalf any releases or other documents that may be required in order to obtain any information,

verbal or written, regarding my physical or mental health.

c. Make all necessary arrangements for health care services on my behalf, including the authority to select, employ and discharge health care providers.

d. Make decisions regarding admission to or discharge from, even against medical advice, any health care facility or service.

e. Sign any documents titled or purporting to be "Consent to Permit Treatment" or "Refusal to Permit Treatment," necessary waivers or releases from liability required by a hospital, physician, or other health care provider.

D. <u>GENERAL INSTRUCTIONS</u>:

To inform those responsible for my care of my specific wishes, I make the following statement of personal views regarding my health care:

Initial ONE of the following two statements with which you agree:

XXX   *1. I direct that all medically appropriate measures be provided to sustain my life, regardless of my physical or mental condition.*

OR

_____   *2. There are circumstances in which I would not want my life prolonged by further medical treatment. In these circumstances, life sustaining measures should not be initiated and if they have been, they should be discontinued. I recognize that this is likely to hasten my death. In the following, I specify the circumstances in which I would forego life-sustaining measures.*

If you have initialed Statement 2, please initial each one of the statements (a, b and c) with which you agree:

a._____ *I realize that there may come a time when I am diagnosed as having a incurable and irreversible illness, disease, or condition. If this occurs, and my attending physician and at least one additional physician who has personally examined me determine that my condition is terminal, I direct that life-sustaining measures which would serve only to artificially prolong my dying be withheld or discontinued. I also direct that I be given all medically appropriate care necessary to make me comfortable and to relieve my pain.*

To me, terminal condition means that my physicians have determined that:
(Check one)
_____ *I will die within a few days*

_____ *I will die within a few weeks*

_____ *I will have a life expectancy of approximately* _____ *or less*
(enter 6 months or one year).

b._____ *If there should come a time when I become permanently unconscious, and it is determined by my attending physician and at least one additional physician with appropriate experience who has personally examined me, and that I have totally and irreversibly lost consciousness and my capacity for interaction with other people and my surroundings, I direct that life-sustaining measures be withheld or discontinued. I understand that I will not experience any pain or discomfort in this condition, and I direct that I be given all medically*

142

appropriate care necessary to provide for my personal hygiene and dignity.

c._____ I realize that there may come a time when I am diagnosed as having an incurable and irreversible illness, disease, or condition which may not be terminal. My condition may cause me to experience severe and progressive physical or mental deterioration and/or a permanent loss of capacities and facilities I value highly. If, in the course of my medical care, the burdens of continued life with treatment become greater than the benefits I experience, I direct that life-sustaining measures be withheld or discontinued. I also direct that I be given all medically appropriate care necessary to make me comfortable and relieve my pain.

(Paragraph c. covers a wide range of possible situations in which you may have experienced partial or complete loss of certain mental and physical capacities you value highly. If you wish, in the space provided below you may specify in more detail the conditions in which you would choose to forego life-sustaining measures. You might include a description of the faculties or capacities which, if irretrievably lost, would lead you to accept death rather than continue living. You may want to express any special concerns you have about particular medical conditions or treatments, or any other consideration which would provide further guidance to those who may become responsible for your care. If necessary, you may attach a separate statement to this document or use Section E to provide additional instructions.)

Examples of conditions I find unacceptable are:

_____

_____

_____

Sample Living Will

E. SPECIFIC INSTRUCTION:

**Artificially   Provided   Fluids   and   Nutrition;
Cardiopulmonary Resuscitation (CPR)**. *On page _____ you
provided general instructions regarding life-sustaining
measures. Here you are asked to give specific instructions
regarding two types of life-sustaining measures - artificially
provided fluids and nutrition and cardiopulmonary resuscitation.*

*1. In the circumstances I initialed on page _____, I also direct
that artificially provided fluids and nutrition, such as feeding
tube or intravenous infusion*

   (Initial one)

   _____ *be withheld or withdrawn and that I be allowed to*
die

   ___**XXX**___ *be provided to the extent medically appropriate*

*2. In the circumstances I initialed on page _____, if I should
suffer a cardiac arrest, I also direct that cardiopulmonary
resuscitation*

   (Initial one)

   _____ *not be provided and that I be allowed to die*

   ___**XXX**___ *be provided to preserve my life, unless medically
inappropriate or futile*

*3. If neither of the above statements adequately expresses your
wishes concerning artificially provided fluids and nutrition or
CPR, please explain your wishes below.*

_____
_____
_____

F. **BRAIN DEATH:**

(The State of _____ recognizes the irreversible cessation of all functions of the entire brain, including the brain stem (also known as whole brain death), as legal standard for declaration of death. However, individuals who cannot accept this standard because of their personal religious beliefs may request that it not be applied in determining their death.)

Initial the following statement only if it applies to you:

_____ To declare my death on the basis of the whole brain death standard would violate my personal religious beliefs. I therefore wish my death to be declared solely on the basis of traditional criteria of irreversible cessation of cardiopulmonary (heartbeat and breathing) function.

G. **AFTER DEATH - ANATOMICAL GIFTS:**

(It is now possible to transplant human organs and tissue in order to save and improve the lives of others. Organs, tissues and other body parts are also used for therapy, medical research and education. This section allows you to indicate your desire to make an anatomical gift and if so, to provide instructions for any limitations or special uses.)

Initial the statements which express your wishes:

_____ 1. I wish to make the following anatomical gifts to take effect upon my death:

_____ A. any needed organs or body parts

_____ B. only the following organs or parts:_____

_____

for the purposes of transplantation, therapy, medical research or education, or

_____ C. my body for anatomical study, if needed

_____ D. special limitations, if any:

_____ 2. I do not wish to make an anatomical gift upon my death.

H. NOMINATION OF GUARDIAN/CONSERVATOR:

If it becomes necessary for a court to appoint a guardian or conservator of my person ("Conservator"), I designate my Agent (or alternate Agent) be appointed as the guardian or conservator of my person.   No bond shall be required of my Guardian/Conservator in any jurisdiction.   Any decisions concerning my health care to be made by my Guardian or Conservator of my person, shall be made in accordance with my directions as stated in this document.

By the use of the term "Guardian" or "Conservator of my person," I mean a person or entity appointed by a court to provide for my care and physical well-being. Such term does NOT include the appointment of a person or entity to manage my financial affairs.

I. HOLD HARMLESS:

All persons or entities who in good faith endeavor to carry out the terms and provisions of this document shall not be liable to me, my estate, or my heirs for any damages or claims arising because of their action or inaction based on this document, and my estate shall defend and indemnify them, except for willful misconduct or gross negligence.

J. SIGNATURE:

By writing this advance directive, I inform those who may become entrusted with my health care of my wishes and intend to ease the burden of decision making which this responsibility may impose. I have discussed the terms of this designation with my Agent and he or she has willingly agreed to accept the responsibility for acting on my behalf in accordance with this directive. I understand the purpose and effect of this document and sign it knowingly, voluntarily and after careful deliberation.

Signed this ____ day of _____, 2000

Signature: _____
Printed Name:_____
Birthdate:_____

K. WITNESS SIGNATURE BLOCK:

Under the penalty of perjury, I declare that the Declarant and each witness signed this document in each other's presence. Based upon my personal observation, the Declarant appears to be a competent individual, and is aware of the nature of this document. The Declarant is personally known to me or has satisfactorily proven to be the person who voluntarily signed this document, and did not appear to be under or subject to any duress, fraud, constraint or undue influence. To the best of my knowledge, I am not:

(1) related to the Declarant by blood, marriage, or adoption,
(2) designated as Agent or alternate Agent under this document,
(3) entitled to any portion of the Declarant's estate according to the laws of intestate succession or under any will or codicil of the Declarant,
(4) the attending physician of the Declarant or an employee of the attending physician or an owner, operator, officer, director, or employee of a hospital or care or residential facility in which the Declarant is a patient or resident,
(5) employee of the Declarant's life or health insurance provider,
(6) directly financially responsible for the Declarant's medical care,
(7) entitled to a present claim against any portion of the Declarant's estate, or
(8) entitled to any financial benefit by reason of the death of the Declarant.

I am at least 18 years of age, and did not sign this document for the Declarant.

Witness Signature: _____

Witness Name: _____

Witness Address: _____

_____

Date: _____

Witness Signature: _____

Witness Name: _____

Witness Address: _____

_____

Date: _____

L. SUBSCRIBER:

State of _____)

) SS.:

County of _____)

Subscribed, sworn to and acknowledged before me by_____, the DECLARANT, and subscribed and sworn before me by _____ and _____, the witnesses, this _____ day of _____ , 2000.

_____

A Notary Public of _____

My Commission Expires

APPENDIX "B"

SAMPLE GENERAL DURABLE POWER OF ATTORNEY

GENERAL DURABLE POWER OF ATTORNEY

I, _____, (hereinafter referred to as "Principal"), presently residing at _____ voluntarily and of sound mind do hereby constitute and appoint, _____, (hereinafter referred to as my "Agent"), residing at_____, my attorney-in-fact to act as hereinafter provided.

My Agent shall have the following powers:

1. To collect, sue for, recover and receive all moneys, interest, dividends, claims and demands now due or that may hereafter become due or belong to me; and to make, execute and deliver receipts, releases and other discharges therefor, under seal or otherwise. This authority shall include the authority to bring appropriate actions for foreclosure of liens or to take any other proceedings authorized by law.

2. To conduct any and all banking transactions as set forth in N.J.S.A. 46:2B-11, to continue or open in my name, bank accounts (savings or checking), in any state or national bank, savings and loan association, or other similar institution, and to continue or open in my name money market accounts or certificates of deposit in any such bank, savings and loan association or other similar institution, and in connection with any such account or accounts:

    (a) To cause checks and moneys to be deposited to my credit therein,

    (b) To endorse my name upon any checks or other instruments of payment made payable to me, for the purpose of depositing the same therein,

    (c) To withdraw funds therefrom, and for that purpose to execute and deliver drafts, withdrawal certificates, checks, or other instruments of payment drawn thereon.

3.   To pay all debts owing by me at any time or times.

4.   To defend, settle, adjust and compromise, all actions, suits, claims or demands whatsoever that are now or may hereafter be pending between me and any person, firm or corporation, in such manner and in all respects as my said attorney-in-fact shall think proper.

5.   To sell any and all shares of stock, bonds or other securities now or hereafter belonging to me and to make, execute and deliver any assignment or assignments of any such shares of stock, bonds or other securities. Such sales may be made at such price or prices and upon such terms as to my said Agent shall be satisfactory, and no person dealing with my said Agent shall be required to question the propriety of her action or to see to the application of the proceeds of any such sale.

6.   To purchase any and all shares of stocks, bonds or other securities which my Agent shall deem proper. No person dealing with my said Agent shall be required to question the propriety of her action or to see to the application of the proceeds of any such purchase.

7.   To vote as my proxy upon all securities of any corporation held or owned by me, at any meeting of stockholders or any corporation, and in particular, but without in any way limiting the generality of the foregoing, to vote on any and all corporate matters, including matters pertaining to the dissolution, merger, consolidation and reorganization of any such corporation, as fully as I might do were I personally present. To consent to or dissent, as she shall deem proper, to or from any corporate action.

8.   To act on my behalf as a partner of any partnership or partnership association, or as a general or limited partner of limited partnership, in which I may have an interest, and to participate in its affairs, including, without limitation, the

dissolution thereof; and to become a member of any partnership, partnership association, or limited partnership (as general or limited partner, or both) and to participate in its affairs, including, without limitation, the dissolution thereof.

9. To enter into, make, sign, execute and deliver, acknowledge and perform any contract, agreement, writing or thing that may, in the opinion of my said Agent, be necessary or proper to be entered into, made or signed, sealed, executed, delivered, acknowledged or performed.

10. To prepare, execute and file all tax returns and reports required by any federal, state or municipal authority, or any agency thereof, and to contest or review by legal proceedings, or in such other manner as my said Agent shall deem advisable, any tax or assessment levied or imposed against or upon me or any property in which I may have an interest, and to settle, adjust and compromise any liability for any tax due to any federal, state or municipal authority, or any agency thereof, upon such terms and conditions as my said Agent shall think fit, including, but not limited to, representation before any office of the Internal Revenue Service, receipt of confidential information and the performance of any and all acts with respect to any such tax matter.

11. To procure and maintain insurance of every kind and character, in order to protect me and my Agent, and any property belonging to me, from loss, injury, damage, liability and the like, and to pay the premiums therefor.

12. To rent safe deposit boxes in her or in my name, and to provide for access thereto by her, or me, or both of us. To employ clerical, stenographic, accounting or legal assistants or attorneys and pay reasonable compensation and fees therefor. To authorize said attorney to help her in carrying out her duties hereunder including, but not limited to, acquiring any banking, investment, financial, social security and pension information.

13. To give, execute, and deliver, in my name or in the name of my said Agent, any and all checks, acknowledgments, agreements and other instruments in writing of whatsoever

nature, as to my said Agent shall seem fit and proper for the carrying on of any of my affairs; to enter into and take possession of any lands, tenements or hereditaments of mine which may be unoccupied or may become vacant or to the possession of which I may be or become entitled, and all and every parcel of real estate belonging to me; for me and in my name and for my use and benefit, to take, receive, and collect any and all rents, issues, and profits of any and all such lands, tenements or hereditaments, and to lease, demise, and farm let the same in such manner as my said Agent shall think fit and proper, and from time to time to renew the leases; to make, execute, sign, seal, acknowledge, and deliver, for me and in my name and as my acts, any and all leases, agreements, or writings which she may deem proper or necessary; to take any ejectment or other judicial proceedings for such purpose as she shall deem proper or necessary; to make or cause to be made any bonds or recognizances; for me and in my name, to engage, hire, and employ any and all kinds of workmen, clerks, assistants, or servants for the better and more effectually enabling my said Agent to conduct and carry on any business or other transactions, and to discharge any and all such workmen, clerks, assistants, or servants now or hereafter employed, engaged, or retained by me; and to order, purchase and contract for such materials and labor as shall be reasonably necessary to preserve, repair and maintain any real or personal property which I now own, or in the future may acquire.

14. To borrow money in my name and for me and in my behalf at any time or from time to time, and if in her discretion she should deem it advisable, to mortgage or encumber any real estate owned or to be owned by me or to pledge or grant a security interest in and to any personal property owned or to be owned by me, under such terms and conditions and for such periods of time as she may deem advisable.

15. To grant, bargain and sell all real estate and personal property (including any and all personal property in my apartment), or any part thereof, now owned or hereafter to be

acquired by me, for such price and on such terms as my said Agent shall deem to be just, right and proper, and, for me and in my name, to make, execute, acknowledge, and deliver good and sufficient bills of sale, deeds and conveyances for the same, either with or without covenants and warranties.

16. To loan or invest money or other of my property to such persons under terms and conditions as my Agent shall deem proper; and to secure such loans or investments in such manner as she may deem advisable.

17. To disclaim, renounce, and forever refuse to accept any and all interest and benefit in and to any property interest to which I may now or hereafter become entitled, whether such property interest would otherwise pass to me under Will, by intestacy or by operation of law. I grant this power notwithstanding that any transaction hereunder may inure to the benefit of my Agent, and consequently, may be affected by a substantial conflict of interest on her part.

18. To make gifts consistent with my usual pattern of giving to one or more "charitable organizations."

19. This Power of Attorney shall not be affected by my disability or incompetence <u>and it shall be equally effective as a copy or an original</u>.

20. All acts done by my Agent pursuant to the power herein granted during any period of my disability or incompetence or uncertainty as to whether I am alive or dead shall have the same effect and inure to the benefit of and bind me, my heirs, devisees and personal representatives as if I were alive, competent and not disabled or incompetent.

21. Without in anyway limiting the foregoing, generally to do, execute and perform any other act, deed, matter or thing whatsoever that ought to be done, executed and performed, or that in the opinion of my said Agent ought to be done, executed or performed, of every nature and kind whatsoever, as fully and effectually as I could do, if personally present.

22. Unless otherwise waived, my Agent shall be entitled to receive as compensation for services rendered in the

administration of my assets, annual commissions on the income and principal of any of my assets subject to such administration by my Agent pursuant to this Power of Attorney, as would be allowed to a non-testamentary trustee under the applicable New Jersey statutes in effect from time to time. Furthermore, my Agent shall be reimbursed from my assets for any expenses she incurs in carrying out her duties as my Agent including, but not limited to, all travel costs incurred when my Agent travels from _____ to New Jersey, child care costs regarding same, hotel costs regarding same, car service costs regarding same and food costs regarding same.

23. All references made and all nouns and pronouns used herein shall be construed in the singular or plural and in such gender as the sense and circumstances require.

24. This Power of Attorney was prepared by Michael A. Weiss, ("Preparer"), Attorney-At-Law, 1373 Broad Street, Clifton, New Jersey 07013 and it immediately, as of the date of execution set forth below (i.e._____, 2000), revokes and replaces any other Power of Attorney I may have executed.

I hereby ratify and confirm all whatsoever my said Agent shall do, or cause to be done, by virtue of this Power of Attorney, and hold harmless my said Agent for any action taken in good faith, without fraud, pursuant to this Power of Attorney. I hereby authorize and direct whoever shall be responsible for my estate or have power over any property of mine to reimburse my Agent for any costs (including legal fees) reasonably incurred by her in or as a result of acting in good faith, without fraud, pursuant to this Power of Attorney.

IN WITNESS WHEREOF, I have hereunto set my hand and seal this _____ day of _____, 2000.

_____
Michael A. Weiss, Esq.
"Preparer"

_____
(Social Security No._____)
"Principal"

_____
(Social Security No._____)
"Agent"

WITNESSES:

Printed Name: _____   Signature: _____
Address: _____
              _____

Printed Name: _____   Signature: _____
Address: _____
              _____

STATE OF NEW JERSEY:
                              :
COUNTY OF _____ :

Subscribed, sworn to and acknowledged before me by _____, the Principal, _____, the Agent, Michael A. Weiss, the Preparer and subscribed and sworn before me by _____ and _____, the witnesses, this _____ day of _____, 2000.

_____
A Notary Public of New Jersey
My Commission Expires

APPENDIX "C"

MANAGED CARE APPEAL CHRONOLOGICAL CORRESPONDENCE

Correspondence of August 25, 1999

August 25, 1999

Michael A Weiss **[REDACTED]**
[REDACTED]
[REDACTED]

Dear Mr. Weiss:

The Grievance Appeal Committee thanks you for your participation during the Grievance Appeal Hearing held on August 19, 1999. The purpose of the Hearing was to discuss your request that claims totalling $**[REDACTED]** for services provided on **[REDACTED]** and **[REDACTED]** by a non-participating provider Dr. **[REDACTED]**, be processed at the in-network benefit level.

The Grievance Appeal Committee has reviewed all information relevant to your request. After carefully considering all documentation submitted and your comments, the Appeal Committee has decided to reverse the original decision. This decision was made on the basis that you were not provided necessary information to access in-network services.

Thank you for your participation in the Grievance Appeal process.

Sincerely,

[REDACTED]

[REDACTED]
for the Grievance Appeal Committee

cc: Grievance Dept.

Correspondence of July 14, 1999 - Page 1

[REDACTED]

July 14, 1999

Michael A Weiss-[REDACTED]
[REDACTED]
[REDACTED]

Dear Member:

We have received your appeal of the decision of the Grievance Committee.

Your appeal is tentatively scheduled to be heard on **August 19, 1999** at our [REDACTED] location. You have the right to attend the hearing and present information to the Appeal Committee regarding your grievance. You may do so in person or via teleconference. Attendance is not mandatory, and your appeal can be heard in your absence. If you are unable to attend on the date specified above, but wish to present your case in person to the Committee, please contact me to reschedule your hearing for the next month's hearing date. *You will have two opportunities to reschedule your hearing. If, after three hearing dates, you still cannot attend, your appeal will be heard in your absence on that third meeting date.*

Please call by **August 11, 1999** to confirm that you wish to have your appeal heard on the above date. If we do not receive confirmation by this date, you will be tentatively scheduled for the following month. I can be contacted at [REDACTED], ext. [REDACTED], Monday through Friday between 9:00 a.m. and 4:30 p.m. to schedule an appointment for your appeal hearing. The time designated is tentative and may vary, depending upon the time needed for the preceding hearing(s). If you intend to

160

Correspondence of July 14, 1999-Page 2

bring an attorney or other representative to the hearing, please notify us at that time.

If you have any additional information to be considered by the Appeal Committee, you may submit it by fax to [REDACTED] or in writing within 7 days of the date of this letter to my attention at [REDACTED], Quality Management Department, [REDACTED], [REDACTED], [REDACTED].

Sincerely,

[REDACTED]
Quality Management

Correspondence of July 7, 1999

[REDACTED]   Grievance Department
                                       [REDACTED]

July 7th, 1999

Michael Weiss
[REDACTED]
[REDACTED]

Dear Mr. Weiss:

We have received your letter of appeal and supporting exhibits sent via certified mail.

You will be advised of the next step in the appeal process in the near future. Your anticipated patience and cooperation is appreciated.

Sincerely,

[REDACTED]
Grievance Department

[REDACTED]

encl

Procedures Governing Appeals Before the [REDACTED]

Grievance Appeal Committee

1. All appeals must be in writing and submitted within 30 days of the date of the notice of the decision of the Grievance Committee.

2. The Appeal Committee will hold an informal hearing to review your appeal. **You have the right to attend the hearing either in person or by teleconference to present your side of the grievance.** Although it is desirable, you are not required to attend the hearing for your appeal to be heard. You may submit additional written information to be considered by the Appeal Committee in lieu of attending the hearing. You may bring any person with you to assist you in presenting your appeal or to provide information in support of your grievance.

3. Grievance Appeal hearings are conducted one day each month. All requests for appeals filed seven working days or more before the hearing day will be heard at that month's hearing. If you are unable to attend the hearing on that day and wish to appear at the hearing, you must call [REDACTED] to reschedule the hearing for the next scheduled hearing day.

4. A notice to you will specify the date of your hearing. You must confirm the date as provided in the notice. Failure to attend the appeal hearing without prior notice to [REDACTED] will result in the appeal hearing proceeding in your absence and a decision being made without your participation.

Grievance Appeal Committee Rules - Page 2

5. Your appeal will be heard by an Appeal Committee comprised of three individuals appointed by the **[REDACTED]** Board of Directors. One of the members will be a non-employee subscriber of **[REDACTED]**.

6. A copy of the information provided to the Appeal Committee will be furnished to you upon request. You may submit additional written information to be considered by the Appeal Committee up to 72 hours in advance of the hearing.

7. The Appeal Committee shall review the decision rendered by the Grievance Committee. In reviewing the decision, it may consider any information presented to the Grievance Committee, as well as any additional information presented by you or **[REDACTED]**.

8. Although the hearing is informal, a record of the hearing will be made by a stenographer. This is done to create an adequate record of the proceeding.

9. The Chair of the Appeal Committee will conduct the appeal hearing. At the beginning of the hearing, a representative of the HMO will summarize your grievance and what has occurred to date, as well as describe the basis of the HMO's continued denial of your grievance. You will also be given a full opportunity to address the Appeal Committee. Your comments should be brief and to the point.

10. You will have the opportunity to question the HMO representative. The Appeal Committee and HMO representative will be able to question you and any other witness you present.

Grievance Appeal Committee Rules - Page 3

11. All testimony will be under oath or affirmation. The Appeal Committee is required to render a decision within 5 working days of the conclusion of the hearing.

12. A lawyer may be present at the hearing to provide counsel and assistance to the Appeal Committee. You have the right to have an attorney attend the hearing and represent you. If you intend to have an attorney at the hearing, you must inform **[REDACTED]** at least 72 hours in advance of the hearing. If you decide to be represented by counsel, **[REDACTED]** may also choose to be so represented.

13. Please remember that the hearing is informal and that there are no formal rights of examination or cross examination. You should not feel intimidated or reluctant to appear before the Appeal Committee and present your side of the appeal.

[REDACTED]
[REDACTED]

Revised 9/8/98

Correspondence of July 1, 1999 - Page 1

MICHAEL A. WEISS
[REDACTED]
[REDACTED]
[REDACTED]

[REDACTED]

July 1, 1999

SENT VIA FAX [REDACTED]
& CERT. MAIL/R.R.R. [REDACTED]

[REDACTED], M.D.
Medical Director
[REDACTED]
Grievance Department
[REDACTED]
[REDACTED]
[REDACTED]

Re: **ID No.** [REDACTED]
Plan Name: [REDACTED]
Plan Type: [REDACTED]
Discogram Consultation/Two (2) Discograms
[REDACTED]
Primary Care Physician: [REDACTED]

Dear Dr. [REDACTED]

Thank you for your letter dated June 10, 1999 (copy attached) regarding your review and recommendations regarding the above. While I sincerely appreciate the time and effort you and your staff dedicated towards addressing and resolving my

166

Correspondence of July 1, 1999-Page 2

concerns, I respectfully request a formal appeal based upon the attached correspondence. More specifically, Exhibit AA is a June 23, 1999 correspondence from my   surgeon, , denoting the medical necessity of the above-mentioned tests. Exhibits BB and CC are my December 7, 1998 and November 20, 1998 letters previously submitted to the Grievance Committee with corresponding attachments.

As there is a large amount of money at stake and I intend to make a clear and convincing argument on my behalf, I respectfully request to be present at said appeal and that said appeal be scheduled on reasonable notice and place. In the interest of being thorough, I have also enclosed a copy of the relevant Explanation of Medical Benefits (see Exhibit DD) regarding the aforementioned determination by the Grievance Committee.

I trust you can appreciate my position and will process my request expeditiously. To that extent, thank you in advance for your cooperation.

Sincerely,

Michael A. Weiss

Correspondence of June 23, 1999 - Page 1

[REDACTED]

[REDACTED]
[REDACTED]

[REDACTED]
[REDACTED]
[REDACTED]

June 23, 1999

[REDACTED]

[REDACTED]
[REDACTED]
[REDACTED]

[REDACTED]
[REDACTED]

[REDACTED]
[REDACTED]
[REDACTED]
RE: WEISS,MICHAEL

To Whom It May Concern:

I am an **[REDACTED]** Provider and saw Michael Weiss on December 3, 1998 for a consultation regarding persistent back pain. During said consultation, Mr. Weiss presented several diagnostic tests which he had undergone in the past six months. Out of all those tests (namely MRIs, x-rays, EMGs, and discograms), the only two that provided positive results for disc degeneration and thus explain the source of Mr. Weiss's pain were the two discograms that had been performed on November 12, 1998 and November 18, 1998 respectively. Based upon the results of these discograms, I immediately recommended that he undergo spinal fusion surgery, which I successfully performed on January 4, 1999. Mr. Weiss is presently doing well and has resumed his normal activities. It is, therefore, my opinion that these tests were medically necessary and the consultation with **[REDACTED]**, who ordered these tests, was also medically necessary. I think it is quite clear that Mr. Weiss has done well following surgery which was really indicated based upon the results of these discograms. Therefore, I think it is imperative that **[REDACTED]** consider these tests a necessary part of his evaluation and payment should be made accordingly.

Thank you for your prompt attention to this matter.

Sincerely yours,

[REDACTED], MD

[REDACTED]

[REDACTED] Grievance Department
[REDACTED]
[REDACTED]
[REDACTED]

June 10, 1999

Michael Weiss
[REDACTED]
[REDACTED]

Dear Mr. Weiss:

Thank you for writing to **[REDACTED]** requesting coverage for services provided by **[REDACTED]** on November 6, November 12 and November 18, 1998. Your concerns have been noted and reviewed by the Grievance Committee.

The referrals that you received for **[REDACTED]** were denied, as these services are only covered in-network with approval to a participating provider. However, after review of the information provided, the claim for November 6, 1998 has been processed in-network and reimbursed to you.

The claims for November 12 and November 18, 1998 have been processed per your out-of-network plan to the provider. When utilizing a non-participating provider without an approved referral, services are covered out-of-network only.

Under the terms of the State-mandated grievance procedure, you have the right to appeal this determination. If you wish to appeal, you must do so within 30 days from the date of this letter. Please submit your appeal in writing, along with any further information that you believe contradicts these findings.

Correspondence of June 10, 1999-Page 2

This information, along with a copy of this letter, should be forwarded to **[REDACTED]** Appeal Committee, **[REDACTED]**.

Sincerely,

[REDACTED], M.D.
Medical Director
[REDACTED]

[REDACTED]

April 27, 1999

Michael A. Weiss
[REDACTED]
[REDACTED]

Dear Michael A. Weiss:

We have received your grievance and appreciate that you have taken the time to let us know your concerns. All grievances are reviewed by our Grievance Committee. This grievance can be identified by reference number **[REDACTED]**. Please be assured that the committee will look thoroughly into this matter and that you will receive a reply from us when a decision has been made.

The Grievance Resolution Process is as follows:

The Grievance Committee shall review and decide the grievance within 30 days of receipt provided no additional information was necessary to resolve the grievance. If there is insufficient information available for a decision to be reached with 30 days, this time may be extended.

A written notice stating the result of the review by the Grievance Committee shall be forwarded by **[REDACTED]** to the member within 10 working days of the date of the decision.

The decision of the Grievance Committee shall be final and binding unless the member appeals in writing to the Grievance Appeal Committee within 30 days of the date of the notice of the decision of the Grievance.

Correspondence of April 27, 1999 - Page 2

You may have a representative from our Member Services Department, with no direct involvement in this matter, assist you in understanding the grievance process. If you would like such assistance, please call the appropriate Member Services number shown on the back of your member ID card.

Sincerely,

Grievance Committee

Correspondence of April 16, 1999 - Page 1

MICHAEL A. WEISS
[REDACTED]
[REDACTED]
[REDACTED]

[REDACTED]

April 16, 1999

SENT VIA CERT MAIL/R.R.R. [REDACTED]
& REGULAR MAIL

[REDACTED], President
[REDACTED]
[REDACTED]
[REDACTED]

    Re: **ID No. [REDACTED]**
            Plan Name: [REDACTED]
            Plan Type: [REDACTED]
            Discogram Consultation/Two (2) Discograms
            [REDACTED]
            Primary Care Physician: [REDACTED]

Dear Mr. **[REDACTED]**:

I sent the attached two (2) correspondences regarding the above-referenced matter to the **[REDACTED]** department. These correspondence are dated **November 20, 1998** and **December 7, 1998**, respectively. I have yet to receive any communication from **[REDACTED]** with respect to same. To

174

that extent, I am beginning to get collection letters and dunning notices from the physician and facilities which rendered the above-referenced services. As I have followed **[REDACTED]** policy and procedures regarding my concerns, I would appreciate the courtesy of a phone call or response letter indicating the particular person responsible for addressing and facilitating these concerns.

As a follow-up, you should know that I underwent successful posterior spinal fusion surgery (with instrumentation and illiac bone graft) on January 4, 1999. Given the successful outcome, I believe the enclosed quite clearly and convincingly articulates my case. In the event I do not receive a formal response from you within thirty (30) days of your receipt hereof, I will begin to facilitate formal legal action against **[REDACTED]** for the full payment of the services rendered plus all costs and fees including reasonable attorney fees. However, I trust this matter can be resolved more amicably. To that extent, I look forward to hearing from you.

Sincerely,

Michael A. Weiss

Correspondence of December 7, 1998 - Page 1

MICHAEL A. WEISS
[REDACTED]
[REDACTED]
[REDACTED]

[REDACTED]

December 7, 1998

SENT VIA CERT> MAIL/R.R.R. [REDACTED]
& REGULAR MAIL

[REDACTED]
[REDACTED]
[REDACTED]
[REDACTED]
[REDACTED]

RE: ID No **[REDACTED]**
    Plan Name: **[REDACTED]**
    Plan Type: **[REDACTED]**
    Discogram Consultation/Two (2) Discograms
    [REDACTED]
    Primary Care Physician: **[REDACTED]**

Dear Sir/Madam:

Enclosed please find a "Medically Necessary" letter from Dr. **[REDACTED]** regarding the two (2) discograms he

Correspondence of December 7, 1998 - Page 2

performed on me on November 12, 1998 and November 18, 1998, respectively. I have also enclosed a copy of my original letter in the interest of facilitating this matter for your files.

I look forward to your response and thank you for your anticipated consideration and cooperation.

Sincerely,

Michael A. Weiss

Correspondence of November 23, 1998 - Page 1

[REDACTED]   November 23, 1998
                                                    [REDACTED]

Mr. Michael Weiss
[REDACTED]
[REDACTED]

[REDACTED]
Re: Letter of Medical Necessity

To whom it may concern,

Please be advised the above mentioned patient was seen and evaluated by me November 6, 1998 for the evaluation and treatment of chronic low back pain. His examination revealed restricted, painful range of motion of the lumbar spine with flexion greater than extension. He has interspinous tenderness, and a positive Larsen's test at the lower lumbosacral levels. His pain has been chronic, severe and disabling and limits his daily activities. It is aggravated by sitting, forward bending and usually not improved with anything.

His diagnostic work-up has been extensive, but inconclusive as to the source of his pain. For this reason, I found it medically necessary to proceed with provocative lumbar discography at the L3-4,L4-5 and L5-S1 levels, followed by CAT scan imaging on November 12, 1998.

CT Discogram revealed the following: L3-4 Normal. L4-5 Partial Annular injection discordant pain. L5-S1 Internal Disco Disruption with concordant low back pain.

Correspondence of November 23, 1998 - Page 2

Due to the partial annular pattern at L4-5, it was recommended to proceed with a repeat Discogram at the L4-5 level, and at the same time administer a trial of intradiscal steroids at the L5-S1 level. This was performed November 18, 1998. My diagnosis is L5 S1 internal disc disruption.

Re: Michael Weiss

Due to Michael's excruciating pain, the repeat Discogram was expedited by scheduling at my **[REDACTED]** N.J. office.

I have referred Michael to a Spine Surgeon for a second opinion.

Should you have any questions regarding this patient, please feel free to contact my office directly.

Sincerely,

[REDACTED]
Physiatrist-in-Chief

Correspondence of November 20, 1998 – Page 1

MICHAEL A. WEISSV
[REDACTED]
[REDACTED]
[REDACTED]

[REDACTED]

November 20, 1998

SENT VIA CERT. MAIL/R.R.R. [REDACTED]
& REGULAR MAIL

[REDACTED]
[REDACTED]
[REDACTED]
[REDACTED]

Re: ID No. **[REDACTED]**
        Plan Name: **[REDACTED]**
        Plan Type: **[REDACTED]**
        Discogram Consultation/Two (2) Discograms
        [REDACTED]
        Primary Care Physician: **[REDACTED]**

Dear Sir/Madam:

The purpose of this letter is to respectfully request that **[REDACTED]** reimburse me in full for treatment I was required to seek outside my Provider Network ("Network") because said treatment was medically necessary but unavailable in the

180

Correspondence of November 20, 1998 - Page 2

Network. I am specifically referring to my November 6, 1998 consultation with Dr. **[REDACTED]** (Telephone Number **[REDACTED]**) at the **[REDACTED]** ("**[REDACTED]**") in New York City (Address **[REDACTED]**) and the two (2) discograms which he performed on Thursday, November 12, 1998 and Wednesday, November 18, 1998, respectively. (Please note that the November 18, 1998 discogram was performed at the **[REDACTED]**, New Jersey (**[REDACTED]**) satellite office of **[REDACTED]** for reasons explained below.)

By way of background, my medical history is as follows: 35 year-old male in good health with no prior back problems. Prior to injuring my back July 4, 1998, my primary health problem consisted of having Crohn's Disease for the past fifteen (15) years in my small intestine which has required approximately seven (7) re-section surgeries and approximately seven (7) related intestinal or incisional surgeries. After looking at my file regarding this back injury, you will undoubtedly become aware of the fact that since approximately July 4, 1998, I have been suffering from what was initially diagnosed as a herniated disc in my back at the "L4/L5" level. To that extent, I have endured numerous diagnostic procedures, taken various muscle relaxers, pain killers and other drugs, undergone physical therapy, and have been to various specialists. Despite these treatments and specialist opinions, the pain in my back, and now down the sides of my legs, has gotten worse - so bad, that since August 1, 1998 I became disabled and unable to work.

Approximately two (2) months ago, my primary care physician, Dr. **[REDACTED]**, **[REDACTED]**, NJ, prescribed an intense course of physical therapy at **[REDACTED]** (**[REDACTED]**). **[REDACTED]** is a member of the **[REDACTED]** Network but was not the physical therapy facility designated by **[REDACTED]** for **[REDACTED]**. Nevertheless,

Correspondence of November 20, 1998 – Page 3

the administrator of my insurance plan procured approval from [REDACTED] because the physical therapy facility assigned to [REDACTED], namely [REDACTED] ([REDACTED]) - [REDACTED], NJ, was inadequate to treat the complexity of my situation. By way of background with respect to that, you should know that I had begun physical therapy at [REDACTED] in July but was forced to stop same when I had a bout with kidney stones in early August. My back had not improved from the treatment at [REDACTED] but after the kidney stones the physicians involved believed my back pain would disappear as it must have been attributed to the kidney stone. However, when I began exercising after passing the kidney stone, the back pain re-emerged. After consultations with various urologists, it was concluded that I did in fact have a back problem and that the kidney stone episode was simply coincidental. The physicians treating my back then recommended I continue physical therapy. As I had kidney stone symptoms during my treatment at [REDACTED] and they were apparently not diagnosed, I was reluctant to resume physical therapy there. Additionally, the interruption of my physical therapy at [REDACTED] because of the kidney stone and my treatment for same exhausted my sixty (60) calendar day physical therapy benefit. As such, the administrator of my [REDACTED] plan and Dr. [REDACTED] fought to get me full physical therapy benefits at [REDACTED]. I am grateful to their efforts and sincerely appreciate [REDACTED] approving the treatment at [REDACTED] as [REDACTED] is one of the most prominent facilities in the world and my case obviously required more expert care than I had been receiving at [REDACTED]. More importantly, [REDACTED] is the facility where I met Dr. [REDACTED] who eventually diagnosed my problem.

Correspondence of November 20, 1998 - Page 4

Despite approximately six (6) weeks of physical therapy at **[REDACTED]**, the pain in my back continued to worsen and included excruciating pain down my legs. To that extent, the physician at **[REDACTED]**, Dr. **[REDACTED]**, felt it medically necessary for me to undergo a "discogram" to determine the "intrinsic disc degeneration" which apparently was the reason my back did not respond to physical therapy. Dr. **[REDACTED]**made this determination on October 31, 1998 and put same in writing in a letter dated November 3, 1998, a copy of which is enclosed (see Exhibit A enclosed). In accordance with the requirements of my coverage with **[REDACTED]**, I met with Dr. **[REDACTED]** on Monday, November 2, 1998, to obtain a referral for said discogram. Despite this specific recommendation from Dr. **[REDACTED]**, Dr. **[REDACTED]** attempted to get me more immediate relief and referred me for a surgical consultation with Dr**[REDACTED]**. The earliest appointment Dr. **[REDACTED]**was able to provide me with was Wednesday, November 5, 1998. Unfortunately, the pain in my back and legs became so severe that I was rushed to **[REDACTED]** Hospital (**[REDACTED]**, NJ) by ambulance the night of November 3, 1998.

I was admitted to **[REDACTED]** Hospital on Monday, November 3, 1998 by Dr. **[REDACTED]**. I was treated with various pain medications and examined by Dr. **[REDACTED]**. Dr. **[REDACTED]**then ordered a MRI test on me which proved negative. At that point I once again explained to Dr. **[REDACTED]** and Dr. **[REDACTED]** that Dr. **[REDACTED]** had requested a discogram which would diagnose my problem as my condition was not being revealed by MRIs, EMGs, Bone Scans or conventional X-Rays. Dr. **[REDACTED]** refused to cooperate as he felt that my problem was not of the surgical nature and therefore not his concern. Dr. **[REDACTED]** however attempted to refer me for a discogram. However, he

Correspondence of November 20, 1998 - Page 5

was unable to provide me with the name of a physician in the Network who performed discograms. Dr. **[REDACTED]** subsequently discharged me from the hospital on Wednesday, November 5, 1998, with medication to make me comfortable and suggested that I find a doctor who would perform a discogram.

After I left the hospital I immediately started calling various neurosurgeons, spine doctors and other physicians that were listed in the **[REDACTED]** Physician Directory who could perform the procedure. Most of the physicians that I contacted had never even heard of a "discogram" and others refused to schedule one since my MRIs and neurological tests were negative. I tried to explain that the "discogram" was designed for exactly such a circumstance but my pleas fell on deaf ears. I then contacted Dr. **[REDACTED]** who suggested several other physicians all of whom were not in the Network. Nevertheless, I contacted these physicians and they were not able to schedule the discogram for at least one (1) month due to busy patient schedules and vacations. I continued to make telephone calls to friends, relatives and physicians I knew and eventually I learned of a physician at **[REDACTED]** named **[REDACTED]** who performed discograms. At this point I had spent two (2) full days making these telephone calls while I battled with excruciating pain and discomfort.

I told Dr. **[REDACTED]** about Dr. **[REDACTED]** and he immediately issued me a referral to get a second opinion and/or discogram from Dr. **[REDACTED]** (see Exhibit B for referrals). I then went to see Dr. **[REDACTED]** on Friday, November 6, 1998 where he examined me. His preliminary diagnosis was that I had a "tear" in one (1) or two (2) discs which needed to be diagnosed and confirmed with a discogram. He then scheduled me for a discogram on Thursday, November 12, 1998. I met with Dr. **[REDACTED]** on Tuesday, November 17, 1998, to go over the results of the discogram. During this office visit he told me

Correspondence of November 20, 1998 - Page 6

that the results of L3/L4 were normal and that the results from L5/S1 revealed that I had mild degenerative disease in that disc. The results from L4/L5 were inconclusive and he recommended that another discogram be performed just on the L4/L5 level to confirm whether I had a problem in just the L5/S1 or if I also had the problem at the L4/L5 level. As part of the second discogram, Dr. [REDACTED] intended to inject steroids directly into the damaged disc or discs. The purpose of this would be to reduce the inflammation and possibly fix the problem. He was unable to do this during the November 12, 1998 discogram because he was required to inject a full amount of saline and dye to diagnose the problem. As I was in excruciating pain and practically unable to walk due to the pain in my legs, Dr. [REDACTED] felt it was medically necessary to perform this procedure as soon as possible. Therefore, I underwent the second discogram at Dr. [REDACTED] [REDACTED], NJ office on Wednesday, November 18, 1998 because that was the earliest appointment he had available. (see Exhibit B for second referral to Dr. [REDACTED] by Dr. [REDACTED]). It is important to point out that Dr. [REDACTED] findings during the discogram clinically explained my symptoms and provided a diagnosis where all other tests had not. The findings confirmed Dr. [REDACTED] determination that the discogram was medically necessary.

During the November 18, 1998 discogram, Dr. [REDACTED] determined that the L4/L5 disc was normal but that the L5/S1 disc was seriously degenerated. (I have enclosed copies of the reports from both discograms - see Exhibit C enclosed). He suspected the source of the degeneration was a deep tear in the disc which is referred to in the second discogram as an "L5 S1 internal disc disruption." To that extent, Dr. [REDACTED] injected steroids into the L5/S1 disc/level. We

Correspondence of November 2, 1998 - Page 7

will know whether the injection of steroids was successful in correcting my problem within three (3) to five (5) days of the injection. However, if it does not work, I will have exhausted every conservative remedy available and will need to pursue some sort of surgical option. Most likely, that option will involve surgically fusing my spine at the L5/S1 level (i.e. Anterior Fusion).

I have enclosed the following invoices for the aforementioned services (see Exhibit D enclosed) which I was required to seek out-of-the Network because they were medically necessary but unavailable in the Network:

1. November 6, 1998 office consultation with Dr. **[REDACTED]** - $325.00 (I paid this amount by charging it to my credit card);
2. November 12, 1998 Discogram performed on three (3) levels - $**[REDACTED]**;
3. November 18, 1998 Discogram and steroid injection - $**[REDACTED]**.

I believe Dr. **[REDACTED]** office submitted the invoices for 2 & 3 above but I have submitted them with this letter so that all three would be considered at the same time that the circumstances were explained in this letter.

I thank you for your anticipated cooperation and assistance. I only pray that you carefully consider my situation and reimburse me for Dr. **[REDACTED]** charges (or pay the remaining charges directly) in the same manner as you would for these services had I been able to receive them in Network. I believe that is the correct application of my **[REDACTED]** policy and it is consistent with the overall fair and compassionate ideology of **[REDACTED]**. To that extent, I look forward to hearing from **[REDACTED]** as soon as possible. (I believe Dr.

Correspondence of November 20, 1998 - Page 8

[REDACTED] office is preparing a "medically necessary" letter which he will sign on Tuesday, November 24, 1998. I will obtain same and forward to you as soon as possible. However, please feel free to call his office to investigate this matter any further as his office is extremely cooperative. His office manager's name is **[REDACTED]**.)

Should you have any questions or require additional documentation, please do not hesitate to contact me.

Sincerely,

Michael A. Weiss

cc: **[REDACTED]**
[REDACTED]
[REDACTED]

Correspondence of November 3, 1998 - Page 1

November 3, 1998

TO WHOM IT MAY CONCERN:

RE: MICHAEL WEISS
    [REDACTED]

    Because of Michael's persistent mechanical back pain and degenerative disc disease shown on MRI and lack of improvement I feel it medically necessary for him to undergo a discogram to determine intrinsic disc degeneration.

    If any additional information is needed, please contact my office at **[REDACTED]**.

Sincerely,

[REDACTED]
[REDACTED], M.D.

About the Author

Michael A. Weiss is a successful and well-respected thirty-eight (38) year old attorney/MBA who unfortunately has been hospitalized more than fifty (50) times due in large part to his seventeen (17) year battle with Crohn's Disease. Crohn's Disease is an "auto-immune" and incurable illness usually causing painful inflammation in the intestines, small bowel and colon. The Disease and its complications have caused Mr. Weiss to undergo numerous abdominal surgeries, hernia surgeries, knee surgery and most recently, serious spine-fusion back surgery. The Disease's "auto-immunity" component has also caused Mr. Weiss to endure comical hospitalizations and emergency room visits for seemingly "run-of-the-mill" ailments such as indigestion, stomach viruses, colds, kidney stones, etc. His somewhat handicapped "recovery" time from these surgeries and afflictions and often-unpredictable medical reaction to prescribed treatments and medications have baffled his physicians and caused him to take the reins on his healthcare.

Mr. Weiss has experienced all of the above in different hospitals, different states, with different doctors and at various stages throughout his life. He has been exposed to interactions with the medical establishment at all levels from the medical, surgical, psychological and rehabilitation wings to the corporate boardroom of stingy managed care companies fighting (and winning!) for coverage and reimbursement. Through it all, he maintained his sense of humor and escaped with his dignity and life intact. While as a young adult he struggled with these problems, he did not let it stop him from pursuing his dream of becoming an attorney and earning a MBA degree. So, while his account of the hospital patient experience is informative and funny, it is also inspirational for patients and their family members. Mr. Weiss hopes his story can also help develop a guide for hospitals and health care workers as to how it and they should carry out their respective responsibilities. Mr. Weiss is also actively involved in established an internet "message board"/network so that hospital patients can talk to one another and find comfort in each other's fears, concerns, hopes and funny stories. If Mr. Weiss is successful, lonely and scared hospitalized children can talk to others around the world at anytime of the day or night simply at the click of a mouse. Mr. Weiss' efforts in this regard begin on the Message Board at http://www.hospitalpatient.com/.

Mr. Weiss currently practices healthcare, elder, business and entertainment law in Clifton, New Jersey. He also often serves as a patient advocate helping patients aged five (5) to ninety-five (95) fight for their rights with respect to hospitalization, physician treatment, managed care and reimbursement issues. He has been a Board Member of the Crohn's & Colitis Foundation of America and is also an adjunct professor at New York's Audrey Cohen College's Executive MBA Program in Media Management lecturing on "Contract Negotiations & Drafting." He frequently writes articles on contractual issues concerning the film, television and internet industries and often lectures on patient/elder rights with respect to care, cost of care, guardianships and nursing home care/cost/planning.